A Moment WITH God

KAY ARTHUR

HARVEST HOUSE PUBLISHERS
Eugene, Oregon 97402

A Special Gift

To

....

From

....

Date

....

....

....

....

....

....

These excerpts were originally published as an inspirational calender under the title *His Imprint, My Expression* by Kay Arthur.

Cover design by Koechel Peterson and Associates, Minneapolis, MN.

A MOMENT WITH GOD
Copyright © 1998 by Kay Arthur
Published by Harvest House Publishers
Eugene, Oregon 97402

ISBN 1-56507-995-7

Printed in China.
98 99 00 01 02 03 04 /IM/ 10 9 8 7 6 5 4 3 2 1 ✳

A Moment with God

January

By My Spirit

*"Not by might nor by power . . . but by My
Spirit," says the* LORD *of hosts.*

ZECHARIAH 4:6

*I*n each of us there is a longing for the spiritual. Because we are not simply body and soul, there's an awareness, a sense of need for something, someone beyond ourselves. Many times we become aware of this when we finally come up against something we cannot control. But what we cannot do, God can—by His Spirit.

REFLECTIONS

Always There for You

When Thou didst say, "Seek My face,"
my heart said to Thee, "Thy face,
O LORD, I shall seek."

PSALM 27:8

*B*eloved, have you ever longed for someone to take you by the hand and walk you safely through the traumas of life? There is One who is always there to listen . . . to guide . . . to mark your life with the imprint of His own. This year, God wants to speak to your heart through His Word and by His Spirit. Will you put your hand in His in childlike trust and say with me, "Yes, Lord . . ."?

REFLECTIONS

God Chose Us!

*He chose us in Him before the
foundation of the world.*

EPHESIANS 1:4

*W*hy *was I born? What is the purpose of my
life?* Have you ever asked yourself these
questions? I was considering them just the
other day. As I did, my mind went to this amaz-
ing truth: Even before God created the heavens
and the earth, He knew you and me, *and He
chose us!* You and I were born because it was
God's good pleasure!

REFLECTIONS

Your Life Has a Purpose

For we are His workmanship, created in Christ Jesus for good works, which God prepared beforehand, that we should walk in them.

EPHESIANS 2:10

Do you realize how absolutely precious you are to God? If you think you aren't or feel differently, you have embraced a lie. You are of value. Your life is significant. It has a purpose. A specific purpose. Not only were you chosen before the world's foundation but God also prepared a plan for your life alone—and neither man nor the devil can destroy that plan.

REFLECTIONS

JANUARY 5

Dependent on God Alone

*In love He predestined us to adoption . . .
through Jesus Christ to Himself, according
to the kind intention of His will.*

EPHESIANS 1:4,5

*C*an I share a secret with you, precious one?
Your worth and purpose do not depend on
what you have done, or what has been done to
you or where you have been, even if you have
been to the very precipice of hell. Your worth
and purpose depend on God and God alone—
His will, His calling, His choosing, His love.

REFLECTIONS

....

....

....

....

....

God's Love for You

In this is love, not that we loved God, but that He loved us and sent His Son to be the propitiation for our sins.

1 JOHN 4:10

Have you begun to grasp the breadth, length, height, and depth of God's love for you? When you were a sinner, ungodly, and without hope, God loved you, pursued you, and wooed you. And He did not let go until you gave in to His desire to be your Father, your Lord, your Redeemer. That is what you are worth to Him.

REFLECTIONS

Choose to Believe God

The sum of Thy word is truth.

PSALM 119:160

Do you sometimes find yourself lost in the maze of the enemy's lies? Your peace, soundness of mind, and effectiveness all depend on what you believe—and *whom* you believe. It does not matter what you feel, think, or hear. If it does not agree with the Word of God, it is a lie. Don't miss knowing your worth and purpose by believing lies of men or the musings of your mind. Choose to believe God.

REFLECTIONS

JANUARY 8

In the Light of God's Grace

I count all things to be loss in view of the
surpassing value of knowing Christ Jesus
my Lord . . . and count them but rubbish
in order that I may gain Christ.

PHILIPPIANS 3:8

Everything you are going through, all that you are dealing with, has one ultimate purpose: that you may know the love of God and live in the light of His extravagant and more-than-adequate grace. You were born for an intimate relationship with God. That is the purpose of your existence. And when you discover that, you'll experience an abiding contentment.

REFLECTIONS

JANUARY 9

Learning to Recognize God's Voice

*And your ears will hear a word behind you,
"This is the way, walk in it," whenever you
turn to the right or to the left.*

ISAIAH 30:21

Do you want an intimate relationship with God? If so, you must consistently and faithfully set aside time so your heavenly Father can communicate with you through His Word and by His Spirit. Talk with Him in prayer. Put yourself in a position for God to meet with you, and everything else will fall into perspective. You will learn to recognize His voice.

REFLECTIONS

Focus on God

For to me, to live is Christ, and to die is gain.

PHILIPPIANS 1:21

Paul wrote these words while a prisoner of Rome. His epistle has come to be known as a letter of joy. Why? How? Both questions are answered in two words, one Person: Jesus Christ. Paul's focus was on Jesus, not on his own life or his circumstances. Where is your focus today? Joy comes when it is Jesus first, others second . . . then you. And if to live is Christ, there's always joy.

REFLECTIONS

Please God Alone

Whom have I in heaven but Thee?
And besides Thee, I desire nothing on earth.

PSALM 73:25

When God is our focus, everything else—including self—has to take a back seat. He is the only One we have to please. Isn't that refreshing? We don't have to be afraid that such an attitude will make us hard or unloving or uncaring. What God works out in our lives will reflect His character, His likeness . . . His imprint.

REFLECTIONS

Seek God's Favor

For am I now seeking the favor of men, or of God? Or am I striving to please men? If I were still trying to please men, I would not be a bond-servant of Christ.

GALATIANS 1:10

When we are set free from the bondage of pleasing others and of pleasing ourselves (and trying to always please others *is* bondage) and when we are free from currying others' favor and others' approval—then no one will be able to make us miserable or dissatisfied. If we know we have pleased God, contentment will be our consolation, for what pleases God will please us.

REFLECTIONS

JANUARY 13

God Holds the Key

*The LORD of hosts has sworn saying, "Surely,
just as I have intended so it has happened,
and just as I have planned so it will stand."*

ISAIAH 14:24

If you are frustrated, Beloved, because something has gone wrong—you did the wrong thing, made the wrong decision—remember God is even sovereign over the contingencies of life. He is the great redeemer, and He can even redeem this one! Confess what you did wrong. He knows your weakness—trust Him and go forward in faith. You will learn, and you will be more conformed to His image. He promises.

REFLECTIONS

Live by God's Power

*For it is God who is at work in you,
both to will and to work for His good pleasure.*

PHILIPPIANS 2:13

Do you want to live a life that pleases God? He has given you the means to do so, Beloved, because in the wonderful mystery of salvation, Christ dwells in you. You are complete in Him. He will meet you right where you are. He does not expect you to have the talents, gifts, or personality of others. You are His unique creation. Now you can live by *His* power, which will work in you and lead you into the good works He has ordained for you.

REFLECTIONS

One Day at a Time

*Commit your way to the LORD, trust
also in Him, and He will do it.*

PSALM 37:5

O Beloved, the will of God is simply that you
submit yourself to Him each day and say,
"Father, Your will for today is mine. Your pleasure for today is mine. Your work for today is
mine." Take one day at a time. *"Tomorrow will
care for itself"* (Matthew 6:34). And remember,
He is God over all your tomorrows.

REFLECTIONS

....

....

....

....

....

His Grace Is Sufficient

Remember, O LORD, Thy compassion and Thy loving kindnesses, for they have been from of old.

PSALM 25:6

When you've failed, do you wonder how things could ever be the same between you and God? Don't you know, precious one, that you belong to the God of all grace? *Grace is the birthright of every child of God.* Grace is there to preserve you in the darkest night of your failures. His grace is sufficient for all your sin, for all your inadequacy, for all your powerlessness.

REFLECTIONS

Unmerited Favor

For by grace you have been saved through faith; and that not of yourselves, it is the gift of God.

EPHESIANS 2:8

*G*race is unmerited favor bestowed on us at the moment of our salvation. The kingdom of heaven is reserved for those who become as little children, for those who look to their Father in loving confidence for every benefit, whether it be for the pardon so freely given or for the strength and power to do His will.

REFLECTIONS

The Lord Is Merciful

Behold, we count those blessed who endured.
You have heard of the endurance of Job
and have seen the outcome of the
Lord's dealings, that the Lord is full
of compassion and is merciful.

JAMES 5:11

*G*race calls you to get up, to throw off your blanket of hopelessness, and to move on through life in faith. And what grace calls you to, grace provides. Grace is power.

REFLECTIONS

....

....

....

....

....

Grace upon Grace

*For of His fulness we have all received,
and grace upon grace.*

JOHN 1:16

O Beloved, how often we seek to live in our own strength and to approach God on our own merit rather than on His grace! We fail to appropriate His grace, which is there to cover our failure and to save us from despair.

REFLECTIONS

JANUARY 20

God's Grace

And He has said to me, "My grace is sufficient
for you, for power is perfected in weakness."
Most gladly, therefore, I will rather boast
about my weaknesses, that the power
of Christ may dwell in me.

2 CORINTHIANS 12:9

We will never cease to need our Father—
His wisdom, direction, help, and support.
We will never outgrow Him. We will always
need His grace. And His grace will never fail. It
is not a well that will run dry, but it is an ocean
whose depths you can never plumb.

REFLECTIONS

....

....

....

....

Grace Saves Us

*But one thing I do: forgetting what lies behind
and reaching forward to what lies ahead,
I press on toward the goal for the prize of
the upward call of God in Christ Jesus.*

PHILIPPIANS 3:13,14

The same grace that saves us is the grace that keeps us. It is not just grace to cover sin, it is grace more than sufficient to overcome *every* sin, *every* weakness. Grace enables us to live as more than conquerors day in and day out, no matter what. There's always grace to begin anew.

REFLECTIONS

Are You Living in Overdrive?

About midnight Paul and Silas were praying and singing hymns of praise to God.

ACTS 16:25

Are you living in overdrive? Life is filled with pressure—pressure to be, pressure to do, pressure to perform, pressure to produce. How can we release the pressures of the accelerated pace of our earthly life so that it doesn't break us? What we hear from the jail cell where Paul and Silas were imprisoned gives us a clue.

REFLECTIONS

Worship Through Music

Yet Thou art holy.

PSALM 22:3

A vital key to releasing the pressures of life is to worship through music. When we worship our Lord and our God in song, we become even more aware of His presence. The tension begins to unravel; the tautness eases; anxieties becomes meaningless, for we are reminded that He is there—our *Jehovah Shammah*, our all-sufficient, sovereign God.

REFLECTIONS

Worship God in Song

I will sing a new song to Thee, O God;
upon a harp of ten strings I will sing
praises to Thee.

PSALM 144:9

o you begin your day in song? Try putting your tape recorder in your bathroom or bedroom. Play a worship tape while you're dressing or listen to Scripture on tape. Sing in the shower. Play music while you do housework or drive to work. You'll find that the words will be engraved on the tablets of you heart and become an everpresent song on your lips.

REFLECTIONS

JANARY 25

Songs of Deliverance

Thou art my hiding place; Thou dost preserve
me from trouble; Thou dost surround
me with songs of deliverance.

PSALM 32:7

*S*inging spiritual songs and making melody
in your heart is God's way of delivering you
from the stresses of the world. The more you
enter into His courts with praise and into His
gates with thanksgiving, the less you will feel
the pressure of daily life.

REFLECTIONS

Joy . . . No Matter What!

But the fruit of the Spirit is love, joy, peace,
patience, kindness, goodness, faithfulness,
gentleness, self-control; against
such things there is no law.

GALATIANS 5:22,23

Did you know that you can have joy, Beloved? Joy . . . a deep, abiding, overriding joy no matter what! It's part of the wellspring of the Spirit for all who will draw from His riches. God's Word assures us that "joy no matter what" can become a reality for us who would grasp this truth and live by the Spirit.

REFLECTIONS

Complete Joy

*If therefore there is any encouragement in
Christ . . . make my joy complete by being of
the same mind, maintaining the same love,
united in spirit, intent on one purpose.*

PHILIPPIANS 2:1,2

*T*he key to having "joy no matter what"
is found in the person of Jesus Christ and in
an attitude that is submissive to His will. The
apostle Paul's joy did not center on freedom
from prison (and prisons take many forms,
don't they?). Rather, his joy was wrapped up in
the person and promises of Christ.

REFLECTIONS

....

....

....

....

....

God's Will

With all boldness, Christ shall even now,
as always, be exalted in my body, whether
by life or by death. For to me, to live
is Christ, and to die is gain.

PHILIPPIANS 1:20,21

It did not matter to Paul whether he was locked up or free. Whatever God wanted to do with the apostle Paul was all right, for Paul's heart and mind were set on one thing: God's will for him. Paul knew that God, not man, held the keys to his prison doors.

REFLECTIONS

....

....

....

....

....

The Perfect Result

*Consider it all joy . . . when you encounter
various trials, knowing that the testing of your
faith produces endurance. And let endurance
have its perfect result, that you may be
perfect and complete, lacking in nothing.*

JAMES 1:2-4

*D*ear friend, whatever you are enduring now
—or whatever comes your way in the
future—it is not without purpose in the sovereignty of God. And it is for that reason,
Beloved, that you can have that inward sense of
joy. God promises that it will not destroy you—
rather, over time it will be the making of you.

REFLECTIONS

Claim Your Joy

*Now I want you to know, brethren, that
my circumstances have turned out for
the greater progress of the gospel.*

PHILIPPIANS 1:12

*H*ave people, things, or circumstances
robbed you of your joy? Pray through
Philippians 1, substituting your circumstances
for Paul's. Make Paul's desire yours. Practice
having his mind-set; claim the joy that will
be yours. And know this: Your joy, in spite of
imprisonment, will be used by God to reach
others.

REFLECTIONS

JANUARY 31

Take God at His Word

And without faith it is impossible to please Him, for he who comes to God must believe that He is, and that He is a rewarder of those who seek Him.

HEBREWS 11:6

Walking in faith brings you to the Word of God, the Balm of Gilead. There you will be healed, cleansed, fed, nurtured, equipped, matured . . . and hear God's "well done" because you have taken Him at His Word. Faith always pleases our God.

REFLECTIONS

February

FEBRUARY 1

Handling the Memories of Failure

For if He causes grief, then He will have compassion according to His abundant loving kindness. For He does not afflict willingly, or grieve the sons of men. To crush under His feet. . . .

LAMENTATIONS 3:32-34

o your failures loom like a dark cloud? Do you find yourself remembering times when you weren't all you should have been, all you could have been? I understand. Such thoughts can be emotionally draining. Turn to the book of Lamentations, and there you'll find hope for handling those haunting failures.

REFLECTIONS

FEBRUARY 2

A God of Love

*The LORD'S lovingkindnesses indeed
never cease, for His compassions never
fail. They are new every morning;
great is Thy faithfulness.*

LAMENTATIONS 3:22,23

God is a God of unconditional, unremitting love, a love that corrects and chastens but never ceases. Therefore, when we fail Him our failures never alter or sway who God is. You can know for a certainty that His compassions are new every morning and His mercies fail not. Even when we are faithless He abides faithful.

REFLECTIONS

....

....

....

....

....

FEBRUARY 3

Teach Me, Lord

*Before I was afflicted I went astray, but now
I keep Thy word. Thou art good and
doest good; teach me Thy statutes.*

PSALM 119:67,68

Let failure be your teacher, not your executioner.

REFLECTIONS

....

....

....

....

....

Handling Failure

"The LORD is my portion," says my soul, "Therefore I have hope in Him."

LAMENTATIONS 3:24

Listen to the infallible Word of God! Hang on to all the promises of God—bring them up against your feelings. Live according to His Word, and eventually you'll find you can handle failure and even benefit yourself and others by dealing with it honestly before God.

REFLECTIONS

....

....

....

....

....

FEBRUARY 5

When Peace Is Gone

Finally, brethren, whatever is true . . .
whatever is right, whatever is pure . . . let your
mind dwell on these things.

PHILIPPIANS 4:8

*H*ave you ever been doing just great, and then someone says something or you remember an incident from the past and suddenly your peace is gone? A cloud of depression begins to overshadow the contentment you felt just moments ago. You must do what God says, Beloved—put away such thoughts. The past is past.

REFLECTIONS

....

....

....

....

....

Changing Thoughts

*We are taking every thought captive
to the obedience of Christ.*

2 CORINTHIANS 10:5

One Sunday our son David came to say good-bye before returning to college. I'd been taking a nap, so I prayed for him and then rolled over to catch another "forty winks." Suddenly the *what ifs* attacked. Had I been the mother I should have been? Had I adequately prepared my son for life? My peace was gone. I allowed myself to anticipate calamity rather than entrust his future to my sovereign God. What will you do when the "What ifs" attack?

REFLECTIONS

....

....

....

....

....

Mental Warfare

*. . . taking up the shield of faith with
which you will be able to extinguish all
the flaming missiles of the evil one.*

EPHESIANS 6:16

Where do thoughts of inadequacy and fear come from? So often we forget that we are in warfare and that Satan's target is our mind. He disguises himself, of course! He doesn't want us to think he has anything at all to do with our thought process. Yet he does. And that is why we are to *take up the shield of faith*.

REFLECTIONS

....

....

....

....

....

Walk by Faith

*God causes all things to work together for good
to those who love God, to those who are
called according to His purpose.*

ROMANS 8:28

*H*ow can we be victorious in mental warfare?
First, when unlovely, untrue thoughts
invade our minds, we must choose to bring
every one of them captive to the obedience of
Jesus Christ. Then we must walk by faith rather
than by our feelings, thoughts, and self-evalua-
tions. No matter what our past, God's Word
holds this sure promise.

REFLECTIONS

....

....

....

....

....

....

Cry to God

I will cry to God Most High,
to God who accomplishes all things for me.

PSALM 57:2

Gracious and holy Father, give me wisdom to perceive You; intelligence to fathom You; patience to wait for You; eyes to behold You; a heart to meditate upon You; and a life to proclaim You, through the power of the Spirit of Jesus Christ, our Lord.

—*Benedict*

REFLECTIONS

....

....

....

....

....

Misery Will Slip Away

Those who love Thy law have great peace,
and nothing causes them to stumble.

PSALM 119:165

The wonderful benefit of living in a way that pleases God is that if you make the will of God your focus day by day, if you seek to please Him alone, you'll find yourself satisfied with life. Misery will slip away like a whipped puppy with its tail between its legs.

REFLECTIONS

....

....

....

....

....

God's Unconditional Love

*I will call those who were not My people,
"My people," and her who was not beloved,
"beloved."*

ROMANS 9:25

I remember the day my life was turned around by Jesus Christ. On July 16, I moved from a religion to a relationship. I saw my sin and my helplessness to change, and acknowledged that Jesus was God and had a right to rule my life. It was then that I was bathed in His unconditional love and experienced forgiveness of my numerous sins. When there was nothing lovely about me, God called me "beloved." If you have not experienced the same . . . do what I did. He wants you as His beloved.

REFLECTIONS

When You Question God's Love

For I am convinced that neither death, nor life, nor angels, nor principalities, nor things present, nor things to come, nor powers, nor height, nor depth, nor any other created thing, shall be able to separate us from the love of God, which is in Christ Jesus our Lord.

ROMANS 8:38,39

*W*hat a truth to cling to when we begin to doubt God's love . . . because of the severity of our pain, the enormity of our loss, the incongruity of the situation. The essence of God's being is love—He never separates Himself from that.

REFLECTIONS

Do You Lack Confidence in God?

And I said, "What shall I do, Lord?"
And the Lord said to me, " . . . You
will be told of all that has been
appointed for you to do."

ACTS 22:10

*D*ear friend, when you don't embrace in faith
what God says about you, you'll find you
lack confidence in God—in His unconditional
love, in His help, in His desire to use you. Your
attention turns to what's wrong in you. How
much better to leave the pit of self-pity, shake
the dust from your past, and move forward in
His promises.

REFLECTIONS

Children of God

See how great a love the Father has bestowed upon us, that we should be called children of God; and such we are. For this reason the world does not know us, because it did not know Him.

1 JOHN 3:1

*I*f I could draw a valentine for you, Beloved, it would be Jesus Christ in the shape of a heart with your picture inside the heart.

REFLECTIONS

....

....

....

....

Forgiveness

*But the lovingkindness of the LORD is from
everlasting to everlasting on those who fear
Him, and His righteousness to children's
children, to those who keep His covenant,
and who remember His precepts to do them.*

PSALM 103:17,18

"In Christ" is a key phrase in the epistles.
However, it maybe that the enemy blinds
you to this truth and whispers in your ear,
"You're no good. You'll never amount to much."
Beloved, if you are God's child, you are no
longer a sinner. You are a saint (one set apart for
God, sanctified). You have received forgiveness
for all your sins—past, present, and future.

REFLECTIONS

A New Creature

*Therefore from now on we recognize no
man according to the flesh; even though
we have known Christ according to the flesh,
yet now we know Him thus no longer.
Therefore if any man is in Christ, he is a
new creature; the old things passed away;
behold, new things have come.*

2 CORINTHIANS 5:16,17

If you are God's child, you are no longer
bound to your past or to what you were.
You are a brand new creature in Christ Jesus.

REFLECTIONS

....

....

....

....

....

Walk in Newness of Life

Therefore we have been buried with Him through baptism into death, in order that as Christ was raised from the dead through the glory of the Father, so we too might walk in newness of life.

ROMANS 6:4

As God's child you are no longer a slave to sin. As a servant of righteousness, you don't have to let sin rule in your body.

REFLECTIONS

Delivered from Darkness

*For He delivered us from the domain
of darkness, and transferred us
to the kingdom of His beloved Son.*

COLOSSIANS 1:13

As God's child, you are no longer part of the kingdom of darkness, but have been seated in heavenly places above all the power of the evil one and his demonic forces.

REFLECTIONS

....

....

....

....

....

Just As You Are

*And because you are sons, God has sent forth
the Spirit of His Son into our hearts,
crying, "Abba! Father!"*

GALATIANS 4:6

As God's child, you are no longer rejected but are accepted in the Beloved—just as you are—because God chose you for Himself before the foundation of the world. You have been adopted as God's dear child and are sealed by His Spirit, who guarantees that you will live with God forever (Ephesians 1:3-14).

REFLECTIONS

....

....

....

....

....

God Has Removed Our Transgressions

As far as the east is from the west, so far has He removed our transgressions from us.

PSALM 103:12

As a child of God, you no longer have to fear the consequences of your past.

REFLECTIONS

....

....

....

....

....

The Lord Is My Helper

He Himself has said, "I will never desert you, nor will I ever forsake you," so that we confidently say, "The Lord is my helper, I will not be afraid. What shall man do to me?"

HEBREWS 13:5,6

As God's child, you no longer have to fear being abandoned, left alone, or left without help.

REFLECTIONS

In the Lord's Hand

Since his days are determined, the number of
his months is with Thee, and his limits
Thou hast set so that he cannot pass. . . .
In whose hand is the life of every living thing,
and the breath of all mankind?

JOB 14:5; 12:10

As a child of God, you no longer have to fear death, for you cannot die before your time. Jesus holds the keys to hell and death. When you die, you will be immediately absent from the body and present with the Lord (Revelation 1:18; 2 Corinthians 5:8,9).

REFLECTIONS

....

....

....

....

....

Draw Near with Confidence

*Let us therefore draw near with confidence to
the throne of grace, that we may receive mercy
and may find grace to help in time of need.*

HEBREWS 4:16

As His child, you no longer need to fear
approaching God. You can come boldly
to His throne and find His mercy—unearned
favor and help—in the time of your need.

REFLECTIONS

....

....

....

....

All Your Needs

And my God shall supply all your needs
according to His riches in glory in Christ Jesus.

PHILIPPIANS 4:19

*A*s God's child, you no longer are to fear not having exactly what you need . . . physically, emotionally, spiritually, materially. God promises to supply all of your needs through Christ Jesus your Lord.

REFLECTIONS

You Belong to Christ

And you belong to Christ;
and Christ belongs to God.

1 CORINTHIANS 3:23

Why not read the New Testament epistles, beginning with Romans, where "in Christ" is a key phrase? Ask God to show you personally who you are in Christ Jesus and what is yours because you belong to Him. If you'll do this, your life will take on a whole new dimension.

REFLECTIONS

Believe!

What then shall we say to these things?
If God is for us, who is against us? He who
did not spare His own Son, but delivered
Him up for us all, how will He not also
with Him freely give us all things?

ROMANS 8:31,32

God loved you—just the way you were—and gave His Son for you. He put you in Jesus Christ and Jesus Christ in you. What more can God do? What more can He say? He's done it all in His Son. He's said it all in His Word. Now, you must do your part: Believe!

REFLECTIONS

....

....

....

....

....

Our God Is Merciful

*Then the LORD passed by in front of him
and proclaimed, "The LORD, the LORD God,
compassionate and gracious, slow to anger,
and abounding in lovingkindness and truth."*

EXODUS 34:6

Our God is not an implacable, rigid, judgmental Father who can never be pleased and who delights to catch us in a fault. How grossly wrong this thinking is! He is merciful, loving, and gracious toward His children.

REFLECTIONS

Run to God

*But it is still my consolation, and I rejoice
in unsparing pain, that I have not
denied the words of the Holy One.*

JOB 6:10

When trials come your way—as inevitably
they will—do not run away. Run to your
God and Father.

REFLECTIONS

....

....

....

....

....

What Is a Christian?

*For all have sinned and fall short of the
glory of God, being justified as a gift
by His grace through the redemption
which is in Christ Jesus.*

Romans 3:23,24

*H*ave you ever thought about what a Christian is? Christians are people who have shuddered at the awfulness of their sin. They have seen sin for what it is: willful rebellion against the rulership of God in their lives. And in turning from their sin, they have embraced God's only means of dealing with sin: Jesus.

REFLECTIONS

March

Stolen Joy

Set your mind on the things above,
not on the things that are on earth.

COLOSSIANS 3:2

"Things" can rob you of your joy. I'll never forget the time I bought a pair of bed sheets on sale, and then couldn't find matching pillowcases. Imagine! I'd try to study or teach and all I could think about were sheets. Ridiculous? Yes. But don't you have your own story of how some insignificant "thing" stole your joy?

REFLECTIONS

....

....

....

....

....

MARCH 2

Christlikeness

But whatever things were gain to me,
those things I have counted as loss
for the sake of Christ.

PHILIPPIANS 3:7

The apostle Paul knew that only one thing could or should be central to him. What was that? Christlikeness. So, he determined that he would develop a single mind by making Christ his goal. To do this, Paul literally had to count everything else as rubbish.

REFLECTIONS

More Like Jesus

*For we who live are constantly being
delivered over to death for Jesus' sake,
that the life of Jesus also may be
manifested in our mortal flesh.*

2 CORINTHIANS 4:11

When we stand before Him, one second in eternity will erase all care or thought of anything except whether or not we allowed the situations of life to make us more like Him. So remember, every situation that requires us to crucify our desires, our reactions, is an opportunity to let people see Jesus in us.

REFLECTIONS

....

....

....

....

....

Fixing Our Eyes on Jesus

Let us also lay aside every encumbrance . . .
and let us run with endurance the race
that is set before us, fixing our eyes on Jesus.

HEBREWS 12:1,2

If I am going to run the race set before me, I must never take my eyes off the goal—and I must run in my lane. What God asks, does, or requires of others is not my business; it is His. I am to be faithful to His calling on my life. He's the one waiting with His reward at the finish line.

REFLECTIONS

MARCH 5

Let It Go

*But whatever things were gain to me,
those things I have counted as loss
for the sake of Christ.*

PHILIPPIANS 3:7

When "things," even things that are cause for celebration or expectation, begin to rob you of His joy, take a careful look at the "thing" in the light of eternity. If it will hinder you from getting on with what God has for you, let it go.

REFLECTIONS

....

....

....

....

Take Every Thought Captive

*We are destroying speculations and every
lofty thing raised up against the knowledge
of God, and we are taking every thought
captive to the obedience of Christ.*

2 Corinthians 10:5

*W*hen something robs you of your peace of
mind, ask yourself if it is worth the energy
you are expending on it. If not, then put it out
of your mind in an act of discipline. Every time
the thought of "it" returns, refuse it.

REFLECTIONS

....

....

....

....

....

A Steadfast Spirit

Create in me a clean heart, O God,
and renew a steadfast spirit within me.

PSALM 51:10

Can you change whatever is robbing you of joy? Turn it around? Rectify it? Live without it? If there is nothing you can do to change it, then be obedient, walk in faith, and forget those things which are behind and press on toward the prize of your high calling in Christ Jesus.

REFLECTIONS

....

....

....

....

Be Content

*I have learned to be content
in whatever circumstances I am.*

PHILIPPIANS 4:11

Yes, Beloved, circumstances can also rob us of our joy. The apostle Paul was well aware of this as he wrote to the believers at Philippi, for he himself was a prisoner of Rome. His circumstances were less than ideal! Yet Paul lived in peace and contentment despite his circumstances. How? Christ was his life. All he wanted was for Jesus to be exalted in his body, whether by life or by death.

REFLECTIONS

....

....

....

....

....

MARCH 9

God Is Eternal

*While we look not at the things which are seen,
but at the things which are not seen; for
the things which are seen are temporal,
but the things which are not seen are eternal.*

2 CORINTHIANS 4:18

Have you ever found yourself distracted—
so busy pursuing earthly things, earthly
pleasures that it has dulled your interest for the
eternal? It's not worth it, Beloved, for the temporal is just that—temporary—and it can dis-
appear in a moment. But the eternal will last
forever.

REFLECTIONS

Rejoice!

*Rejoice in the Lord always;
again I will say, rejoice!*

PHILIPPIANS 4:4

Do you want to know a sure way to have victory and peace in the midst of any situation? Rejoice! The minute you begin rejoicing, your circumstances cease to control you. The command to rejoice does not mean rejoicing in your circumstances; it means rejoicing in your Savior who is Lord over every circumstance.

REFLECTIONS

....

....

....

....

....

A Matter of Obedience

*I, Nebuchadnezzar, raised my eyes toward heaven,
and my reason returned to me, and I blessed the
Most High and praised and honored Him who
lives forever. . . . He does according to His will
in the host of heaven and among the inhabitants
of earth; and no one can ward off His hand
or say to Him, "What hast Thou done?"*

DANIEL 4:34,35

Are you in a predicament? You could not be
where you are without the Lord's fore-
knowledge. God is sovereign: He rules over all,
nothing happens without His permission.
Rejoicing is a matter of obedience—an obedience that will start you on the road to peace and
contentment.

REFLECTIONS

....

....

....

....

Live by Faith

*I can do all things through
Him who strengthens me.*

PHILIPPIANS 4:13

We are to live by faith, not feelings. To paraphrase Paul's words: "I can keep on bearing all things through Him who constantly infuses His strength into me." Christ's strength, His grace, His power are sufficient to enable us to endure whatever comes our way.

REFLECTIONS

....

....

....

....

....

Be Strong and Courageous!

Have I not commanded you? Be strong and courageous! Do not tremble or be dismayed, for the LORD your God is with you wherever you go.

JOSHUA 1:9

What does it mean to be strong and courageous? To be strong is to refuse to be weak—weak in trust, weak in conviction, weak in obedience. To be courageous is to step out in faith—to trust and obey, no matter what.

REFLECTIONS

....

....

....

....

....

Jesus Is Watching

Let your forbearing spirit
[sweet reasonableness] be known
to all men. The Lord is near.

PHILIPPIANS 4:5

O my friend, what do you do when you feel "out of sorts" with others? Let them have it? Or at least let them know it? Don't! Jesus is there watching, and He's sufficient.

REFLECTIONS

....

....

....

....

....

Rejoice, No Matter What!

*Discipline yourself for
the purpose of godliness.*

I Timothy 4:7

No matter what our circumstances, we can rejoice and let our forbearing spirit be known to all, receiving from our Lord the power to do so and accepting that power in faith, remembering He is at hand!

REFLECTIONS

....

....

....

....

....

Anxious for Nothing

Be anxious for nothing, but in everything by prayer and supplication with thanksgiving let your requests be made known to God.

PHILIPPIANS 4:6

The world will tell you that it is natural and normal to be anxious. Well, anxiety may be natural and normal for the world, but it is not to be part of a believer's lifestyle!

REFLECTIONS

Look First to God

Be anxious for nothing, but in everything by
prayer and supplication with thanksgiving let
your requests be made known to God

PHILIPPIANS 4:6

The moment anxious thoughts invade your mind, go to the Lord in prayer. Look first to God. Rehearse His character, His promises, His works. Remember His names, His attributes, and how they apply to your situation. You will see the cause of your anxiety in a whole new light.

REFLECTIONS

....

....

....

....

....

Live by God's Word

Do not be anxious for tomorrow.

MATTHEW 6:34

ear friend, don't be anxious in the midst of today, and don't become anxious thinking about tomorrow. God, who rules over today, rules over tomorrow. He neither slumbers nor sleeps so He's there at the stroke of midnight, ready to care for you.

REFLECTIONS

....

....

....

....

....

Trials

*We are afflicted in every way, but not crushed;
perplexed, but not despairing. . . . For we who
live are constantly being delivered over to
death for Jesus' sake, that the life of Jesus also
may be manifested in our mortal flesh.*

2 CORINTHIANS 4:8,11

Yes, we are tempted on every hand. The world is appealing. To one degree or another, our lives will be filled with disappointments, discouragements, defeats, difficulties. God's Word calls these "trials." Yet God says that trials are for our good; they are intended to make us more like Jesus.

REFLECTIONS

Salvation

The wind blows where it wishes and you hear
the sound of it, but do not know where it
comes from and where it is going;
so is everyone who is born of the Spirit.

JOHN 3:8

*A*ren't you just awed at the mystery of salvation? One minute a person is lost, and the next minute he or she is saved! You don't see anything spectacular or mysterious taking place; and yet, all of a sudden, the person is a brand-new creature in Christ Jesus, indwelt by the Spirit of God because he has been born again.

REFLECTIONS

....

....

....

....

....

Thanksgiving

And the peace of God, which surpasses all comprehension, shall guard your hearts and your minds in Christ Jesus.

PHILIPPIANS 4:7

The act of thanksgiving is a demonstration of the fact that you are going to trust, to believe God. Thanksgiving is where faith comes in. And what is the end result? Peace instead of anxiety.

REFLECTIONS

....

....

....

....

Lasting Fruit

*Even so, every good tree bears good fruit; but
the bad tree bears bad fruit. . . . So then,
you will know them by their fruits.*

MATTHEW 7:17,20

How can you tell the professors—those who merely name the name of Christ—from the possessors—those who are truly indwelt by Him? According to the Word of God, true Christianity brings forth lasting fruit—the evidence of salvation. For the next week we'll be doing some fruit inspecting!

REFLECTIONS

....

....

....

....

....

A Person's Walk

*If we say that we have fellowship with Him
and yet walk in the darkness, we lie
and do not practice the truth.*

1 JOHN 1:6

The first fruit that gives evidence of a genuine faith is a person's walk. A Christian walks the way Jesus walked, ordering his or her behavior accordingly. Jesus is the light of the world. He did not walk in darkness—and neither can those who are His true followers.

REFLECTIONS

....

....

....

....

....

Habitual Sin

*And you know that He appeared in order to
take away sins; and in Him there is no sin.
No one who abides in Him sins [present
tense in the Greek; implying continuous
or habitual action]; no one who sins
has seen Him or knows Him.*

1 JOHN 3:5,6

A true Christian does not live in habitual sin.
Oh, yes, we do commit singular acts of
sin, but sin—a life lived independently of God—
cannot be the habit of our lives!

REFLECTIONS

....

....

....

....

....

Continued Pereverence

*They went out from us, but they were not
really of us; for if they had been of us,
they would have remained with us; but
they went out, in order that it might be
shown that they all are not of us.*

Another evidence of genuine faith is continued perseverance. Can a person be saved
and then turn away from what he or she once
professed as clearly set forth in the Word of
God? No. Mark it well, Beloved: True believers
do not permanently stray from God.

REFLECTIONS

....

....

....

....

MARCH 26

Love of Others

The one who says he is in the light and yet hates his brother is in the darkness until now. . . .We know that we have passed out of death into life, because we love the brethren.

1 John 2:9; 3:14

A true Christian cannot help but love others. Love of others is evidence of a genuine faith. Because love is an attribute of God, and because a Christian is a person who is indwelt by God, then it is only logical that love would be a fruit that a child of God would bear!

REFLECTIONS

....

....

....

....

....

Overcomers

*For whatever is born of God overcomes the
world; and this is the victory that has overcome
the world—our faith. And who is the one
who overcomes the world, but he who
believes that Jesus is the Son of God?*

1 JOHN 5:4,5

ead Jesus' messages to the churches in
Revelation 2–3. Look at the rewards given
to overcomers and you'll see that true believers
are overcomers. Because Christ is in us and because He, by the Holy Spirit, enables us to keep
His commandments, we are able to overcome
the world!

REFLECTIONS

God's Abiding Spirit

*By this we know that we abide in Him
and He in us, because He has
given us of His Spirit.*

1 John 4:13

*A*nother evidence of genuine faith is the inward witness of the Spirit of God (Romans 8:14-16). If a person has the witness of the Spirit in his heart, he will also have all the other evidences of salvation. These manifestations of genuine Christianity will be evident to one degree or another throughout the Christian's sojourn here on earth.

REFLECTIONS

....

....

....

....

....

A Thirst for Righteousness

Blessed are those who hunger and thirst for righteousness, for they shall be satisfied.

MATTHEW 5:6

Once the Holy Spirit moves in a person's heart —convicting of sin, righteousness, and judgment—there is an awakening of a thirst for righteousness, a longing to be finished with sin and its awful harvest. Then, when in salvation the Holy Spirit takes up His residence within a child of God, the Spirit causes him to set his mind on the things of the Spirit (Romans 8:1-8).

REFLECTIONS

Hungry for God's Word

*Now we have received, not the spirit
of the world, but the Spirit who is
from God, that we might know the
things freely given to us by God.*

1 Corinthians 2:12

How can you tell the saved from the lost? The saved are hungry for His Word and His righteousness. This is the seventh evidence of genuine faith. It is the Spirit of God within us who not only gives us a hunger for God's Word, but also enables us to understand the things of God. The veil comes off when Christ comes in!

REFLECTIONS

....

....

....

....

Choose Jesus

*I have been crucified with Christ. . . . And the
life which I now live in the flesh I live
by faith in the Son of God, who loved me,
and delivered Himself up for me.*

GALATIANS 2:20

Jesus Christ alone is to be my one desire—
His life, not mine. I am to love Him above
all else, above all others. And when choices are
to be made, I am to choose Him above all others. After all, Jesus is Lord. He is God. He is
the have preeminence in my life.

REFLECTIONS

....

....

....

....

April

Wait for the Lord

Wait for the LORD; be strong, and let your heart take courage; yes, wait for the LORD.

PSALM 27:14

*A*re you hanging on by your fingernails, dear one? If I didn't know what I know about God, I might tell you to call it quits and to get on with your life. But because God is who He is, because our times are in His hands, I have to tell you not to give up. Don't "get on with your life." Wait, wait, I say, for the Lord, for His direction, His solution. He's never late.

REFLECTIONS

....

....

....

....

....

Sit at His Feet

*Martha, Martha, you are worried and bothered
about so many things; but only a few
things are necessary, really only one, for
Mary has chosen the good part, which
shall not be taken away from her.*

LUKE 10:41,42

How do you "wait for the Lord?" First you must learn to sit at His feet and take time to "listen to His words." Martha, who was eager to "do for the Lord," was distracted from Him by her preparations for the Lord—by her 'much serving.' This can easily become so true of us. It's noticeable when we start criticizing others and thinking the Lord doesn't care about us!

REFLECTIONS

The One Needful Thing

*Cease striving [let go, relax]
and know that I am God.*

PSALM 46:10

Beloved, sitting at Jesus' feet and listening to His Word is a choice. Some things will not get done. Some people will not understand. But Jesus said it was the one needful thing—the one thing which could never be taken away. Because of what you learn from Him and of Him, you'll always have something to hang onto—and it won't be by your fingernails!

REFLECTIONS

....

....

....

....

....

God's Will Alone

*Every word of God is tested;
He is a shield to those who
take refuge in Him.*

PROVERBS 30:5

Another part of waiting on the Lord is telling God that you want only what He wants—whatever that is. Does that sound terrifying? Not if you make it a practice to do the first thing: Sit at His feet and know Him.

REFLECTIONS

....

....

....

....

....

No Other Agenda

*For am I now seeking the favor of men, or
of God? Or am I striving to please men?
If I were still trying to please men, I would
not be a bond-servant of Christ.*

GALATIANS 1:10

If you will give God your reputation, if you will seek no agenda other than God's, if you are willing to do His will no matter the cost, then His life will be your life . . . and your life, His!

REFLECTIONS

....

....

....

....

....

Do It!

*Trust in the LORD with all your heart, and
do not lean on your own understanding.
In all your ways acknowledge Him,
and He will make your paths straight.*

PROVERBS 3:5,6

If you are making a habit of sitting at Jesus' feet, then whatever God says to you, do it with confidence and without hesitation.

REFLECTIONS

....

....

....

....

....

Set Apart
unto God

*. . . who has saved us, and called us with a
holy calling, not according to our works, but
according to His own purpose and grace which
was granted us in Christ Jesus from all eternity.*

2 TIMOTHY 1:9

Holy, means to be set apart unto God.
Another word for holy is "sanctified."
This means that because God has set us aside
for Himself, our lives—all that we are and do—
are to be set apart for Him.

REFLECTIONS

Eternal Dividends

For you have been bought with a price: therefore glorify God in your body.

1 CORINTHIANS 6:20

*E*ven our bodies are not our own. . . . We cannot do with them as we want and please God. If we sow to the flesh, we will reap corruption. But if we sow to the Spirit, we will reap eternal dividends.

REFLECTIONS

Holiness Is Possible!

You shall be holy, for I am holy.

1 PETER 1:16

Precious child of God, if God says you are to be holy, then holiness is possible! Are you investing in those things which build up, nurture, and edify? Or in those things which are going to snare you, entrap you, or make you ashamed?

REFLECTIONS

Make Time for God

*And it was at this time that He went off
to the mountain to pray, and He spent
the whole night in prayer to God.*

LUKE 6:12

There are so many people naming the name of Christ who do not make time for God—time to get to know Him . . . time to meet with Him daily . . . time to pray . . . time to study His Word. Their time is consumed by self—then it's gone, never to be redeemed, because it hasn't been spent on eternal values. Even Jesus made time to be alone with the Father.

REFLECTIONS

Redeem the Time

*Therefore be careful how you walk, not as
unwise men, but as wise, making the most
of your time, because the days are evil.*

EPHESIANS 5:15,16

God commands us to redeem the time—
to buy it back, to control it and not to let it
control us—because the days are evil. God
wants us to invest our time and energies in
things that have eternal value and in people
whom He created for Himself, not in things
which are useless, temporal, self-centered, or
destructive!

REFLECTIONS

What About Money?

*Let your character be free from the love of
money, being content with what you have;
for He Himself has said, "I will never
desert you, nor will I ever forsake you."*

HEBREWS 13:5

*B*eloved, we've talked about time—what
about money!? What are you doing with
your money? Are you spending it on earthly
treasures or are you making eternal invest-
ments? Have you prayed about your resources
lately? Find out how God wants you to use your
time and your money. No matter what it costs,
forsake all that is not of God.

REFLECTIONS

....

....

....

....

Walk Circumspectly

He has told you, O man, what is good;
and what does the LORD require of you
but to do justice, to love kindness,
and to walk humbly with your God?

MICAH 6:8

How my heart is burdened by the awful harvest so many are reaping . . . the pain, the destruction they've fallen into—and the futility of it all! How we need to take a good look at what we are doing with our lives, our time, our energies, our bodies. As beloved children, we must be vigilant and walk circumspectly.

REFLECTIONS

Losers?

If anyone wishes to come after Me,
let him deny himself, and take up his cross daily,
and follow Me.

LUKE 9:23

Do you ever feel like a loser as a Christian? It happened to my husband and me when our oldest son turned to the world for help, rather than God. We looked like losers. We were denounced as losers and those who were associated with us were to be most pitied. I thought my heart would break . . . until God took me to the cross. Now that son is saved! The world couldn't help—but Jesus did.

REFLECTIONS

The Untold End

*Therefore you too now have sorrow; but I will
see you again, and your heart will rejoice,
and no one takes your joy away from you.*

JOHN 16:22

Suspended between heaven and hell, Jesus
was taunted, rejected, cursed. So much had
been expected of Him. So much proclaimed. Yet
there He hung—raw, beaten, bloody, gasping for
breath. He looked like a loser, but the end of
His story hadn't been told . . . and neither,
Beloved, has the end of your story or mine!

REFLECTIONS

....

....

....

....

....

God's Message of Victory

*Therefore, since Christ has suffered in the flesh,
arm yourselves also with the same purpose,
because he who has suffered in the flesh
has ceased from sin, so as to live the rest
of the time in the flesh no longer for the
lusts of men, but for the will of God.*

1 PETER 4:1,2

The cross takes care of the past. The cross takes care of the flesh. The cross takes care of the world with its lusts and boastful pride. The cross is God's means of victory. It is also the path of ministry.

REFLECTIONS

Winners

*And Thou hast made them to be a
kingdom and priests to our God;
and they will reign upon the earth.*

REVELATION 5:10

We belong to Jesus, and Jesus belongs to God! We have been made part of a kingdom of priests who will reign with Him when He comes to earth again as King of kings and Lord of lords. As children of God, we are winners, simply by faith in our Lord Jesus Christ!

REFLECTIONS

Free Indeed!

*If therefore the Son shall make you free,
you shall be free indeed.*

JOHN 8:36

All the world's counsel won't set you free from sin. In fact, people may call you "an addict." Sin is addictive. But Jesus came to set us free, to redeem us from the slave market of sin—and that's what He'll do for you. So give up, Beloved, and turn your life over to Him.

REFLECTIONS

....

....

....

....

....

APRIL 19

The Sanctuary of God!

When I pondered to understand this, it was troublesome in my sight until I came into the sanctuary of God; then I perceived their end.

PSALM 73:16,17

In Psalm 73, the psalmist tells how envious and discouraged he was when he looked at the apparent prosperity and ease of the wicked. Bitterness crept into his life—until he went into the sanctuary of God. There is a payday, someday.

REFLECTIONS

Communing with God

*When my heart was embittered . . . I was like a
beast before Thee. Nevertheless I am continually
with Thee; Thou hast taken hold of my right
hand. With Thy counsel Thou wilt guide me.*

PSALM 73:21-24

"In the sanctuary" is an Old Testament metaphor for communing with God. The Tabernacle was a sanctuary where God dwelt among His people. God wanted them to see that all life was to be centered around communion with Him. Why? Because without His perspective, our Father knows we always end up in frustration, confusion, or destruction.

REFLECTIONS

APRIL 21

A Proper Perspective

*For the word of God is living and active
and sharper than any two-edged sword, and
piercing as far as the division of soul and spirit,
of both joints and marrow, and able to
judge the thoughts and intentions of the heart.*

HEBREWS 4:12

In the sanctuary, in our communion with God, we gain a proper perspective of life. As we thoughtfully read and meditate on the Word of God, moving through it book by book, God speaks to us. His words, His precepts become a measurement, a divine assessment for our own lives—our values, our desires, our behavior . . . and what we are to think and believe.

REFLECTIONS

....

....

....

....

Do You Need Strength?

Strength and beauty are in His sanctuary.

PSALM 96:6

Precious one, have you ever thought, "It would just be easier to die"? That thought entered my mind one day. But because I live in the Word, I knew it was not from God. Satan is the liar, a murderer. So I ran to the sanctuary of God's presence and there received strength to go on . . . strength to resist, to persist. What about you? Do you need strength?

REFLECTIONS

Discovering Beauty

O God, Thou art awesome from Thy sanctuary
The God of Israel himself gives strength and
power to the people. Blessed be God!

PSALM 68:35

In the sanctuary we discover beauty: the
beauty of His presence, the beauty of His
person, the beauty of His purpose for our life.
In the sanctuary we know His imprint. Then
in the world we become an expression of who
He is.

REFLECTIONS

The Nearness of God

But as for me, the nearness of God is my good;
I have made the Lord GOD my refuge.

PSALM 73:28

Knowing God's unlimited sovereignty and unconditional love imparts a beauty to life . . . and to YOU. Lines of stress, wrinkles of frustration, creases of bitterness are lifted from your face as you quietly, unhurriedly sit before your God . . . reading His Word, stopping to pray, sorting things out, confessing, and listening. Then you can say Psalm 73:28 with the psalmist.

REFLECTIONS

....

....

....

....

....

Answers to Our Problems

*I know whom I have believed and I am
convinced that He is able to guard what I
have entrusted to Him until that day.*

2 TIMOTHY 1:12

As I listen to others and review my own life,
I am more and more convinced that the
answers to our problems are not found in "four
principles of this and that" or in positive con-
fession and positive beliefs (note that I said
positive, not proper!) but in an intimate, knowl-
edgeable relationship with our Father God and
our Lord and Savior Jesus Christ.

REFLECTIONS

Surrounded by Skeptics?

*Flesh and blood did not reveal this to you,
but My Father who is in heaven.*

MATTHEW 16:17

Are you surrounded by skeptics? Dear friend, don't try to defend God! Simply explain Him as the Word of God explains Him. It's your responsibility to give them the Word. It is God's responsibility to open their eyes and turn them from darkness to light.

REFLECTIONS

....

....

....

....

....

God Is Infinite

Woe to the one who quarrels with his maker—an earthenware vessel among the vessels of earth! Will the clay say to the potter, "What are you doing?"

ISAIAH 45:9

Is it hard for you when a skeptic points out man's inhumanity toward man and asks where God is? Skeptics don't understand. Our God is infinite. He sees all, knows all, and is eternal. He allows evil (Isaiah 45:7). He can intervene and many times He does, but only when it fulfills His eternal purpose.

REFLECTIONS

Jesus Is Coming

*The Lord is not slow about His promise,
as some count slowness, but is patient
toward you, not wishing for any to perish
but for all to come to repentance.*

2 PETER 3:9

For so long now, so many have looked for and talked about the second coming of Jesus Christ. Generations have lived in that expectation. But He still hasn't come. Have we put our hopes on a myth? Oh, no! It's just that there are yet some to be added to His invisible church, the company of believers, the bride of Christ. Be patient, and stay alert. He'll come any day now, and you want to be ready.

REFLECTIONS

Walk On in Faith

The vision is yet for the appointed time;
it hastens toward the goal, and it will not fail.
. . . The righteous will live by his faith.

HABAKKUK 2:3,4

The prophet Habakkuk was frustrated by the deep sin and corruption surrounding him. What was his recourse? God—and God is enough. So, Beloved, like the prophet we must lay our questions, anxieties, and impotence at the feet of God and walk on—in faith. Judgment is coming; so is Jesus.

REFLECTIONS

Do Not Fear!

*Do not fear! Stand by and see
the salvation of the LORD.*

EXODUS 14:13

I do not know your specific trial or frustration, my friend. I do not know the anxieties of your battle. But God does and you are precious to Him. What you do not understand, what you feel unable to cope with, can be overcome moment by moment if you will live by faith, taking God at His word and seeking His direction in prayer.

REFLECTIONS

....

....

....

....

....

May

Unbelief Is Sin!

In everything give thanks; for this is
God's will for you in Christ Jesus.

1 THESSALONIANS 5:18

Many of us know today's Scripture backward and forward, but it's hard to believe we should give thanks when we cannot see any earthly reason for what has happened! Yet, my friend, hard or not, when we do not give thanks, we are walking in unbelief. And unbelief is sin!

REFLECTIONS

....

....

....

....

....

God Is in Control

The mind of man plans his way,
but the LORD directs his steps.

PROVERBS 16:9

Do you ever think, "I missed it!" Maybe you did, but could it be that God had something else in mind? I must admit I was a little stressed when I missed a connecting flight in Philadelphia. If I had been in control, I wouldn't have missed the plane! *However, I would have missed what God had in mind*—a precious flight attendant who needed Jesus.

REFLECTIONS

....

....

....

....

....

Give Thanks in Everything

*For as high as the heavens are above the
earth, so great is His lovingkindness
toward those who fear Him.*

PSALM 103:11

*B*ecause our sovereign God is never out of
control, because He rules over all—the
small and the big things of life, the tragedies
and triumphs—and because He loves us with
an everlasting love—we can give thanks in
everything.

REFLECTIONS

MAY 4

The Coming of the Lord

For you yourselves know full well
that the day of the Lord will come
just like a thief in the night.

1 THESSALONIANS 5:2

Suppose, just suppose, that you knew the coming of the Lord was near. Suppose you knew for certain that soon you would be standing before your God, giving an account of how you have lived as His child. Would it make a difference in the way you live today? Next month? Are you making the most of the time He's given you?

REFLECTIONS

....

....

....

....

Be Careful How You Walk

Therefore be careful how you walk,
not as unwise men, but as wise.

EPHESIANS 5:15

id you know that we are accountable to God for all of these things? What we have been given (Matthew 25:1-30). What we know (Luke 12:4-48). Our stewardship of God's Word (1 Corinthians 4:1-5). What we teach others (James 3:1; 1 Corinthians 3:10-15). Our giving (Philippians 4:14-17). Our words (Matthew 12:36,37). And our leadership (Hebrews 13:17).

REFLECTIONS

"I'm Accountable"

*Has the LORD as much delight in burnt
offerings and sacrifices as in obeying the voice
of the LORD? Behold, to obey is better than
sacrifice, and to heed than the fat of rams.*

1 SAMUEL 15:22

*T*oday, would you turn back to the Scriptures
listed in yesterday's thought? Look them up,
one by one, mark them in your Bible in a special
way, or write "I'm accountable" in the margin
next to the verse. Then ask God to search your
heart in each area in the light of His Word. If
you'll do this, God will imprint these in your
mind.

REFLECTIONS

....

....

....

....

....

Set Specific Goals

*So teach us to number our days, that we
may present to Thee a heart of wisdom.*

PSALM 90:12

*I*n the light of what you learned yesterday,
why not set some specific goals for your life?
For instance because you are accountable to
God for knowing His will and for doing it, you
may need to plan how you are going to make
the time to be alone with Him in His Word so
that He can speak to you.

REFLECTIONS

....

....

....

....

....

MAY 8

Formulate Definite Plans

*The Lord GOD has given me the tongue of
disciples, that I may know how to sustain the weary
one with a word. He awakens me morning by morning, He awakens My ear to listen as a disciple.*

ISAIAH 50:4

As you set your goals, formulate definite plans
to reach them. For instance, to follow
through on yesterday's example of making time
to be with God, schedule your day to allow yourself uninterrupted time to be alone with Him.
It's best to begin the day in His Word, at His feet.

REFLECTIONS

....

....

....

....

....

Take Action

*For even though I am absent in body,
nevertheless I am with you in spirit,
rejoicing to see your good discipline
and the stability of your faith in Christ.*

COLOSSIANS 2:5

Once you have set goals and made your plans, begin! It's been said that it takes 21 days of repetition to form a habit. So determine that for the next 21 consecutive days you are going to take time to be alone with God and in His Word.

REFLECTIONS

....

....

....

....

....

Days of Cleansing

*Therefore, since we have so great a cloud of
witnesses surrounding us, let us also lay aside
every encumbrance, and the sin which so
easily entangles us, and let us run with
endurance the race that is set before us.*

HEBREWS 12:1

Now, begin examining every other aspect
of your life in the light of His coming.
The days ahead will become days of cleansing
as you put away those things—sins, habits, possessions, activities, and excesses that encumber
you and keep you from pursuing His holiness.

REFLECTIONS

....

....

....

....

Eternal Dividends

Therefore, my beloved brethren, be steadfast,
immovable, always abounding in the work
of the Lord, knowing that your toil
is not in vain in the Lord.

1 CORINTHIANS 15:58

*S*omeday Jesus will appear. It could be tomorrow or years away. Whenever, Beloved, you are to be waiting and watching, not sleeping—but occupied until He comes. Your diligence will pay eternal dividends. When Jesus comes, He'll bring your reward with Him (Revelation 22:12).

REFLECTIONS

....

....

....

....

My Stronghold

My soul waits in silence for God only;
from Him is my salvation. He only is my
rock and my salvation, my stronghold;
I shall not be greatly shaken.

PSALM 62:1,2

Has God ever seemed so distant that the joy of His presence seemed lost to you? Heaven is silent. Winter has set in. Your heart shivers. It is in these times that we draw on all that we have learned from His Word, all that we know of His character and His ways, and blanket ourselves in these truths.

REFLECTIONS

....

....

....

....

MAY 13

God's Purpose Is Victory

Neither death, nor life, nor angels, nor
principalities, nor things present, nor things to
come, nor powers, nor height, nor depth,
nor any other created thing, shall be able
to separate us from the love of God,
which is in Christ Jesus our Lord.

ROMANS 8:38,39

*E*ven when we cannot hear him, God's purpose is always victory, not defeat. He has
not abandoned us, the work of His hands. Oh,
no! God will never separate Himself from one
of His children.

REFLECTIONS

Periods of Silence

Who is among you that fears the LORD, that obeys the voice of His servant, that walks in darkness and has no light? Let him trust in the name of the LORD and rely on his God.

ISAIAH 50:10

In any intimate relationship there are always periods of silence. God may be silent because He has spoken and we have not responded—so He waits. Or His silence may be a test of our faith. Whatever His reason, we can rely on God—even in His silence.

REFLECTIONS

Cling to God's Promises

Unto thee will I cry, O LORD my rock;
be not silent to me.

PSALM 28:1 (KJV)

When God is silent we must steep ourselves in His Word and cling to His promises. Cling, until He breaks the silence. There is always a reason for what God does—a purpose under heaven. And when He does break the silence, our relationship with Him will be more treasured than before.

REFLECTIONS

This Precious Truth

He Himself has said, "I will never desert you,
nor will I ever forsake you," so that we
confidently say, "The Lord is my helper,
I will not be afraid."

HEBREWS 13:5,6

*W*hen we walk with God in the silent times, He becomes all that matters—not our emotions, not our desires, not our pleasures. We begin to walk in meekness, accepting everything as coming from God without murmuring, disputing, or retaliating. This precious truth becomes ours.

REFLECTIONS

God Is There

*Now to Him who is able to keep you from
stumbling, and to make you stand in the
presence of His glory blameless with great joy,
to the only God our Savior, through Jesus
Christ our Lord, be glory, majesty,
dominion and authority.*

JUDE 24,25

Whether we feel God's watch-care or not,
whether we sense His presence or not, He
is there—never ceasing to love us with His
everlasting love and never failing to cause all
things to work together for our good. God is
never to point to your defeat; rather, He's there
to make sure you succeed.

REFLECTIONS

A Good Work Perfected

*He who began a good work
in you will perfect it until
the day of Christ Jesus.*

PHILIPPIANS 1:6

W hat God begins, God completes.

REFLECTIONS

In This Life We Are Expendable

But even if I am being poured out as a drink offering upon the sacrifice and service of your faith, I rejoice and share my joy with you all.

PHILIPPIANS 2:17

We human beings don't handle rejection very well. When persecution and trials come, our natural tendency is to wonder what we have done wrong to bring us into such painful difficulty. We forget—or perhaps we've never learned—that in this life we are expendable for the sake of the furtherance of the gospel.

REFLECTIONS

Never Apart from His Love

Who shall separate us from the love of Christ?

ROMANS 8:35

At times the Lord may seem distant, far away, unreachable. But you are never apart from His love, His promises, from Himself. Silence? It's possible. Separation? Absolutely impossible.

REFLECTIONS

A Glorious Day

For now we see in a mirror dimly, but
then face to face; now I know in part,
but then I shall know fully
just as I also have been fully known.

1 CORINTHIANS 13:12

What a day, what a glorious day it will be when Jesus Christ returns. Never again will there be a feeling of distance between you and your Lord. Never again shall a doubt of His love violate your faith. Hallelujah!

REFLECTIONS

....

....

....

....

....

MAY 22

There All the Time

And He shall wipe away every tear from their eyes; and there shall no longer be any death; there shall no longer be any mourning, or crying, or pain; the first things have passed away.

REVELATION 21:4

Someday we shall dwell in sweet union and communion with our God and Savior forever and ever. The final silence will be broken, and we will see Him as He is . . . as He has been . . . there all the time.

REFLECTIONS

....

....

....

....

....

Digging Diligently

How blessed are those who observe His testimonies, who seek Him with all their heart.

PSALM 119:2

Diligently digging into God's Word book by book will take the "ho hum" out of your relationship with Him. Ask God what book of the Bible you ought to study. Then start by asking questions. Who is the book about, what are its main themes, when was it written, where did the events take place, why is this book (chapter, verse) important?* You'll be awed at what you learn.

*The International Inductive Study Bible is designed for this type of study and includes instructions to help you get the most out of Scripture.

REFLECTIONS

....

....

....

....

....

A Multitude of Distractions

The counsel of the LORD stands forever, the plans of His heart from generation to generation.

PSALM 33:11

I know, precious one, that life in today's world offers a multitude of distractions. But don't let them rob you of intimacy with God. Don't let them rob you of the power of God in your daily life. You'll deeply regret it if you do— for you'll find yourself unprepared for life's contingencies.

REFLECTIONS

Make God Your Priority

My soul languishes for Thy salvation;
I wait for Thy word.

PSALM 119:81

Intimacy with God and holiness come when you make God your priority . . . when you get into His Word and wait on Him to speak to you . . . when you wait until, in the inner man, you know He is saying, "This is the way, walk in it."

REFLECTIONS

MAY 26

....

Before God
in Prayer

*In the morning, O LORD, Thou wilt hear
my voice; in the morning I will order my
prayer to Thee and eagerly watch.*

PSALM 5:3

*W*here do you gain great confidence in
God and in His will for you each day of
your life? In waiting before Him in prayer.
Because your goal is not simply to know God's
Word, but to know the God of the Word and
roll every care, every concern, every question,
every need onto His shoulders.

REFLECTIONS

....

....

....

....

....

Searching for the Heart of God

And you will seek Me and find Me,
when you search for Me with all your heart.
And I will be found by you.

JEREMIAH 29:13,14

Don't you want to know your God so intimately that your heart touches His—that your hearts beat as one? Prayer is searching for the heart of God to know and do His will, to sense and share His love, to hear and intercede for others.

REFLECTIONS

....

....

....

....

....

Be Still

And after the earthquake a fire;
but the LORD was not in the fire:
and after the fire a still small voice.

1 KINGS 19:12 (KJV)

We must learn to do more than pray, "Bless me . . . give me . . . help me." We must meditate on His Word, be quiet before Him— still enough to hear His voice . . . and obey.

REFLECTIONS

Seek to Be Holy

*How can a young man keep his
way pure? By keeping it according
to Thy word. With all my heart I have
sought Thee; do not let me wander
from Thy commandments.*

PSALM 119:9,10

God is looking for men, women, teens, and children who will tremble at His Word—for those who will respect Him as God and treat Him accordingly. Those who will believe Him . . . obey Him . . . honor Him as God . . . worship Him in accordance with all that He is. Will you be that person, Beloved?

REFLECTIONS

Embrace God's Cross

*Always carrying about in the body
the dying of Jesus, that the life of Jesus
also may be manifested in our body.*

2 CORINTHIANS 4:10

Does joy seem a stranger to you? Maybe it's because you haven't embraced God's cross in your life. The words of Josif Trif, a 66-year-old Romanian pastor, explain it so clearly, "If it weren't for Communism, I would not have loved our Lord as much. I kissed the cross the Communists gave me."

REFLECTIONS

Kiss Your Cross

*And he who does not take his cross and
follow after Me is not worthy of Me.*

MATTHEW 10:38

O Beloved, if you are lacking peace or joy, it might be because you are failing to walk in the sweetness of faith's obedience. Kiss your cross—it's from His sovereign hand. There's a purpose in it all . . . your Christlikeness.

REFLECTIONS

June

Satan's Five Deadly D's

*Your adversary, the devil, prowls about like a
roaring lion, seeking someone to devour.*

1 PETER 5:8

*H*as disappointment ever caused you to go into an emotional tailspin? Have you ever felt you might drown in discouragement? Then, my friend, you have engaged in warfare with the evil one and allowed him to penetrate your line·of defense. Let's take a look at how you can be more than a conqueror over Satan's Five Deadly D's: disappointment, discouragement, dejection, despair, and demoralization.

REFLECTIONS

The First Deadly D

But as for me, I trust in Thee,
O LORD, I say, "Thou art my God."
My times are in Thy hand.

PSALM 31:14,15

The first deadly D is Disappointment. To counterattack disappointment you need to launch the Christian's Strategic Defense System—faith that in meekness praises God in every situation by seeing it as God's sovereign appointment.

REFLECTIONS

....

....

....

....

....

The Second Deadly D

Have I not commanded you? Be strong and coura-
geous! Do not tremble or be dismayed, for the
LORD your God is with you wherever you go.

JOSHUA 1:9

The second deadly D is Discouragement.
After Moses died, God was careful to ad-
monish Joshua to "be strong and courageous."
Years earlier the Israelites believed the report
of the spies who became discouraged by the
giants in the land God had given them to occupy.
So they wandered in the wilderness for 40
years! What about you? Have you listened to
the world's analysis of your condition rather
than courageously believing your God?

REFLECTIONS

....

....

....

....

The Third Deadly D

*But as for me, I will hope continually, and
will praise Thee yet more and more.*

PSALM 71:14

*H*ave you ever found yourself mired in the
mud of Dejection? Instead of the joy of
the Lord being your strength (Nehemiah 8:10),
you are about to faint (Isaiah 61:3). When dejection pulls you down into its depths, reach up
and take hold of His hand with the act of praise.

REFLECTIONS

The Fourth Deadly D

Why are you in despair, O my soul? And why
have you become disturbed within me?
Hope in God, for I shall again praise Him
for the help of His presence.

PSALM 42:5

The fourth deadly D is Despair—to despair is to lose or abandon hope. Despair leaves you apathetic, your mind is numb. O precious child of God, when you are in despair, look for a specific promise of God to counter each cause of despair. Then you will find yourself saying Psalm 42:5 with the psalmist.

REFLECTIONS

JUNE 6

The Final Deadly D

*For God hath not given us the spirit
of fear; but of power, and of love,
and of a sound mind.*

2 TIMOTHY 1:7 (KJV)

The final deadly D is Demoralization. Demoralized people run in circles—if they have the strength to run! They cannot get their act together in any of the disciplines of life. Many times they are simply paralyzed with fear. But God has not given you a spirit of fear, rather a sound mind—a mind under control. God loves you. If you are His child, you have His power. Use it.

REFLECTIONS

....

....

....

....

....

Happiness and Joy?

*But even if I am being poured out
as a drink offering upon the sacrifice
and service of your faith, I rejoice
and share my joy with you all.*

PHILIPPIANS 2:17

We are living in a time of unprecedented selfishness. Today the rallying cry is "Be number one." But when being number one is our goal, then everyone else must be in second place—including God. Is this what happiness and joy are all about?

REFLECTIONS

....

....

....

....

....

JUNE 8

A Servant Mind

Have this attitude in yourselves [or, "let this mind be in you"] which was also in Christ Jesus, who, although He existed in the form of God, did not regard equality with God a thing to be grasped, but emptied Himself, taking the form of a bond-servant.

PHILIPPIANS 2:5-7

The mind of Christ is a servant mind.

REFLECTIONS

....

....

....

....

....

Are You Willing?

*But I thought it necessary to send to you
Epaphroditus, my brother and fellow worker
and fellow soldier, who is also your messenger
and minister to my need; because he was
longing for you all and was distressed because
you had heard that he was sick.*

PHILIPPIANS 2:25,26

Are you concerned for the spiritual welfare
of others? Are you willing to give yourself
to listening to them, to helping them, to meeting their needs, to showing them what God has
to say in His Word? Oh, how we need to say,
"Here am I, Lord. Use me. Send me."

REFLECTIONS

....

....

....

....

....

Don't Lose Heart

*Fixing our eyes on Jesus, the author and
perfecter of faith, who for the joy set before
Him endured the cross, despising the shame,
and has sat down at the right hand of the
throne of God. For consider Him who has
endured such hostility by sinners
against Himself, so that you may not grow
weary and lose heart.*

HEBREWS 12:2,3

Sometimes the joy of obedience does not
bring immediate results. It is then we must
be reminded of the much greater burden our
Lord bore in humbling Himself unto death.

REFLECTIONS

Losing Your Joy

*For even the Son of Man did not come
to be served, but to serve, and to give His life
a ransom for many.*

MARK 10:45

It is not people who rob us of our joy; it is our failure to have the mind of Christ. When you start to lose your joy because of people, stop and ask God, "How would You have me serve You in this situation—right now?"

REFLECTIONS

....

....

....

....

....

God Is Faithful

*God is faithful, who will not allow you to be
tempted beyond what you are able, but with
the temptation will provide the of escape
also, that you may be able to endure it.*

1 CORINTHIANS 10:13

Today's Scripture, Beloved, is your assurance
that God will never permit anything to come
your way that you cannot handle. Whatever the
trial, testing, or temptation, you can know that
if it were not possible for you to endure it in a
way pleasing to your heavenly Father, He would
not permit it.

REFLECTIONS

....

....

....

....

....

God Does Not Tempt Us

Let no one say when he is tempted,
"I am being tempted by God"; for God
cannot be tempted by evil, and He
Himself does not tempt anyone.

JAMES 1:13

*I*f we think the source, the hotbed, of temptation is God, we're deceived. God is altogether holy and would not tempt us to do evil!

REFLECTIONS

....

....

....

....

....

The Source of Temptation

But each one is tempted when he is carried
away and enticed by his own lust.

JAMES 1:14

God wants you to realize that temptation does
not come from without, but from within.
Oh, the opportunity to sin is always there;
however, it is not the world or the devil that
causes you to be tempted—it is your own flesh!

REFLECTIONS

JUNE 15

Child of Desire

*He who is steadfast in righteousness
will attain to life, and he who pursues
evil will bring about his own death.*

PROVERBS 11:19

Sin is a child of desire. Recognize your desires for what they are. If you rationalize them and accommodate them, you will find yourself right in the middle of sin.

REFLECTIONS

Walk in the Spirit

*But I say, walk by the Spirit, and you will
not carry out the desire of the flesh.*

GALATIANS 5:16

God does not say that our flesh will not have
desires. Rather, He says that the flesh and
the Spirit "are in opposition to one another"
(Galatians 5:17), and because of this tension,
you cannot just do as you please. You must con-
sciously choose to walk in the Spirit.

REFLECTIONS

The Cravings of the Flesh

What is the source of quarrels and conflicts among you? Is not the source your pleasures that wage war in your members?

JAMES 4:1

Don't make the mistake of thinking of desires as "needs." God promises to supply all your needs (Philippians 4:19). Needs are never contrary to His Word, but desires are the cravings of your flesh.

REFLECTIONS

....

....

....

....

....

Flee from Lust

Now flee from youthful lusts, and pursue
righteousness, faith, love and peace,
with those who call on the Lord
from a pure heart.

2 TIMOTHY 2:22

You are never above temptation because it is your own lust—your own flesh—which entices you, and you will have to live with that flesh until you see the Lord. Flee from lust. In the power of the Spirit get out of there fast and get far away.

REFLECTIONS

Your On-Call Comforter

And He will give you another Helper
[Comforter], that He may be with you forever.

JOHN 14:16

*A*re you in a battle? Does a "Goliath" loom before you? Look up! Look up to the heavens, up to your Father's throne, up to your High Priest standing at the right hand of the Father on your behalf. Then look within! Is the Spirit of the living God not dwelling within? Is He not your resident Helper, your on-call Comforter?

REFLECTIONS

....

....

....

....

Divinely Powerful Weapons

*The weapons of our warfare are not
of the flesh, but divinely powerful
for the destruction of fortresses.*

2 CORINTHIANS 10:4

Stop and think about the story of David and Goliath. The Israelites facing Goliath had the same God on their side that David had on his. What made the difference? They trusted in "the arm of flesh"—thus they were defeated! *David trusted in what he knew about God.* Who are you trusting?

REFLECTIONS

JUNE 21

The Lord of Hosts

*You come to me with a sword, a spear,
and a javelin, but I come to you
in the name of the LORD of hosts.*

1 SAMUEL 17:45

When David faced Goliath, he remembered that God was *Jehovah-sabaoth*, the Lord of hosts, which means He is the Captain of all—all principalities, powers, and spiritual forces in high places. Why do we fear Satan when we're on God's side?

REFLECTIONS

....

....

....

....

....

Proving Your Faith

Therefore, strengthen the hands that are
weak and the knees that are feeble.

HEBREWS 12:12

O Beloved, don't you see? God in His sovereignty permits "Goliaths" in your life as tests . . . tests which give you an opportunity to prove your faith. And in proving your faith, you prove Him and, thus, are strengthened.

REFLECTIONS

No Way Out

*I know, O my God, that Thou triest the
heart and delightest in uprightness.*

1 CHRONICLES 29:17

You'll never be the Christian you can be
without "Goliaths." You'll never know God
intimately apart from them. It's the trials, the
conflicts, the adversities, the "no way out" situations, the impossibilities that drive us to God,
where we discover who He is and what He is.

REFLECTIONS

....

....

....

....

....

Run "into His Name"

The name of the LORD is a strong tower;
the righteous runs into it and is safe.

PROVERBS 18:10

I pray that you'll get to know your God by
name and that in the day of adversity you'll
not hesitate to call upon the name of the Lord,
that you'll not hesitate to run "into His name"
and be secure.

REFLECTIONS

....

....

....

....

Consider It All Joy

Consider it all joy, my brethren,
when you encounter various trials,
knowing that the testing of your faith
produces endurance.

JAMES 1:2,3

*W*e seem to associate only blessings with
the goodness of God. How earthbound
we are! How temporal our perspective! To the
child of God, even trials are cause for rejoicing!

REFLECTIONS

"Follow Me!"

*Jesus said to him, "If I want him to
remain until I come, what is
that to you? You follow Me!"*

JOHN 21:22

*H*ave you ever looked at another Christian
and thought, "They've got it made!
They're so blessed of God!" After Jesus told
Peter how he was going to suffer and die, He
said to him, "Follow Me!"(John 21:19). Peter,
seeing his fellow disciple John, asked Jesus
what was going to happen to him. Do you know
what Jesus replied?

REFLECTIONS

You Are Uniquely You

*. . . . that the proof of your faith, being more
precious than gold which is perishable,
even though tested by fire, may be found to
result in praise and glory and honor
at the revelation of Jesus Christ.*

1 PETER 1:7

*B*eloved, you are not the same as any other
person! You are uniquely you. So God has a
unique, individual set of circumstances which
He will use to refine and purify you so that you
will come through the fire of affliction with the
dross of your ungodliness consumed.

REFLECTIONS

Blessings in Disguise

In this you greatly rejoice, even though now for a little while, if necessary, you have been distressed by various trials.

1 PETER 1:6

To consider it all joy is to look down the long road to the eternal . . . to look beyond the trial to the end result, which is you, perfect and complete, lacking nothing. Trials are blessings in disguise.

REFLECTIONS

Nothing Is Hidden

*For it is time for judgment to begin
with the household of God; and if
it begins with us first, what will
be the outcome for those who do
not obey the gospel of God?*

1 PETER 4:17

Nothing is hidden from God. We cannot pretend to be righteous on the outside while inside we are filled with unrighteousness. We can be sure our sin will find us out. The justice of God, the righteousness of God, the very character of God requires it—and will see to it!

REFLECTIONS

JUNE 30

....

God's Grace Is Sufficient

And He has said to me, "My grace is sufficient for you, for power is perfected in weakness." Most gladly, therefore, I will rather boast about my weaknesses, that the power of Christ may dwell in me. Therefore I am well content with weaknesses, with insults, with distresses, with persecutions, with difficulties, for Christ's sake; for when I am weak, then I am strong.

2 CORINTHIANS 12:9,10

God's grace is not only available, it is sufficient.

REFLECTIONS

....

....

....

....

July

How Much Do You Hate Evil?

You have wearied the LORD with your words. Yet you say, "How have we wearied Him?"

MALACHI 2:17

How much do you hate evil? Some Christians think themselves magnanimous when they say, "There is a little bit of good in everyone, and we need to see the good. After all, God does!" Does He? Listen to how we weary God: Malachi goes on to say, "In that you say 'Everyone who does evil is good in the sight of the Lord, and He delights in them.'" We weary God when we don't agree with Him regarding evil. When we excuse sin that God must deal with. We weary God because when we do things like this we diminish His holiness.

Your Only Allegiance

Should you help the wicked and love those who hate the LORD and so bring wrath on yourself from the LORD?

2 Chronicles 19:2

Doesn't today's Scripture pose an interesting question? How would you answer it, Beloved? What is your alliance with the ungodly? What is your allegiance to them? Your only allegiance ought to be the love of God that would mourn over their sin and seek to rescue them from judgment.

REFLECTIONS

God Never Compromises

Wash yourselves, make yourselves clean;
remove the evil of your deeds from My
sight. Cease to do evil, learn to do good;
seek justice, reprove the ruthless; defend
the orphan, plead for the widow.

ISAIAH 1:16,17

Compromising men and women may call evil good in the sight of the Lord and say that God delights in them, but that is a lie. God never compromises with evil; He only exposes evil for what it is and then judges it. Remember, Beloved, you serve a holy God.

REFLECTIONS

JULY 4

Pray for Our Land Today!

First of all, then, I urge that entreaties and prayers, petitions and thanksgivings, be made on behalf of all men, for kings and all who are in authority, in order that we may lead a tranquil and quiet life in all godliness and dignity.

1 TIMOTHY 2:1,2

Pray for our land today!
Intercede for our leaders.
Pray that men and women will turn from their wickedness and bow in godly repentance.
Plead for God's mercy.

REFLECTIONS

....

....

....

....

Someone to Intercede

And I searched for a man among them
who should build up the wall and
stand in the gap before Me for
the land, that I should not destroy it;
but I found no one.

EZEKIEL 22:30

*H*as it ever occurred to you that God could use your earnest prayers to change the course of our nation's history? Israel's cup of iniquity was full. Over and over God had called His people to repentance, but they would not listen. Can you hear the anguish in His voice as He looks for someone to intercede?

REFLECTIONS

....

....

....

....

....

Clothe Yourself in God's Armor

*No man has authority to restrain the wind with
the wind, or authority over the day of death;
and there is no discharge in the time of war,
and evil will not deliver those who practice it.*

ECCLESIASTES 8:8

If we diligently intercede for our nation, perhaps God will stay His hand of judgment and bring revival. Beloved, now is not the time to be sleeping. Now is the time to use our weapons of warfare. Clothe yourself in His armor, take up the weapons He has given you, and fight the good fight of faith.

REFLECTIONS

Pray Diligently

"Woe is me, for I am ruined! Because I am a man of unclean lips, and I live among a people of unclean lips. . . ." Then one of the seraphim flew to me, with a burning coal in his hand which he had taken from the altar with tongs. And he touched my mouth with it and said, "Behold, this has touched your lips; and your iniquity is taken away, and your sin is forgiven."

ISAIAH 6:5-7

As you begin to pray diligently, God will use your intercession to make you more like the man or woman of God you long to be. You can't be in His presence praying earnestly and not be changed!

REFLECTIONS

....

....

....

....

Cast Your Care on God

Surely I have composed and quieted my soul;
like a weaned child rests against his mother.

PSALM 131:2

It's hard to trust God when the "forecast" is contrary to what we feel we need, isn't it? Maybe it's a restored relationship, and the forecast is grim. Maybe it's a job, and the outlook is bleak. What do you do? What can you do? You can cast all your care on the One who cares for you.

REFLECTIONS

God's Mighty Hand

*Thou hast a strong arm; Thy hand
is mighty, Thy right hand is exalted.*

PSALM 89:13

God has you in His hand, and His hand is a mighty hand. Mighty not only to save and to keep, but mighty to deliver. He brought the children of Israel "out of Egypt with a mighty hand, when they cried to Him" (Deuteronomy 9:26; Exodus 2:23-25). Can He not also deliver you with His mighty hand?

REFLECTIONS

The Lord Is My Helper

Let your character be free from the love of money, being content with what you have; for He Himself has said, "I will never desert you, nor will I ever forsake you," so that we confidently say, "The LORD is my helper, I will not be afraid. What shall man do to me?"

HEBREWS 13:5,6

*H*as God not promised to "supply all your needs according to His riches in glory in Christ Jesus" (Philippians 4:19)? God is immutable; He cannot change. He cannot lie. He will not leave you nor forsake you.

REFLECTIONS

....

....

....

....

God Cares for You

Humble yourselves, therefore, under the mighty hand of God, that He may exalt you at the proper time, casting all your anxiety upon Him, because He cares for you.

1 PETER 5:6,7

*B*eloved, roll that burden, that care, that anxiety, that weight off your back and onto God's almighty shoulders. You are the sheep of His pasture, and sheep are not burden-bearing animals! He cares for you. He cares for you. (Have you got that?! He cares for you.)

REFLECTIONS

Cry to God

*Who among all these does not know that
the hand of the LORD has done this,
in whose hand is the life of every living
thing, and the breath of all mankind?*

JOB 12:9,10

He is God! Cry to Him. If it is for your good and His glory, God will answer your cry. If not, He won't, because what He has planned is better. The plans God has for you are plans for good and not for evil, to give you a future and a hope (Jeremiah 29:11).

REFLECTIONS

God Hates Divorce

"I hate divorce," says the LORD,
the God of Israel.

MALACHI 2:16

*H*as there ever been a time, even for one
second, when you have thought it might
be nice to be divorced? How I appreciate those
who, though living with mates who are talking
about divorce, desire to know what God says
about it in His Word and act accordingly. Our
marriages and commitment to one another are
to be earthly pictures of Jesus Christ's unconditional, sacrificial love for His bride, the church.

REFLECTIONS

Marriage Is a Covenant

Husbands, love your wives, just as Christ also loved the church and gave Himself up for her.

EPHESIANS 5:25

Do you know why God hates divorce? First, because marriage is a covenant, and covenants are not to be broken. God made a covenant with Israel. He also made a covenant with the church, the new covenant in Jesus' blood, which grants us grace that leads to eternal life. He'll never break that covenant.

REFLECTIONS

....

....

....

....

Divorce Distorts

For this cause a man shall leave his father and mother, and shall cleave to his wife; and the two shall become one flesh. This mystery is great; but I am speaking with reference to Christ and the church.

Ephesians 5:31,32

The second reason God hates divorce is that marriage is a picture of our covenant union with the Lord Jesus Christ. Earthly marriages are to be a picture of our heavenly marriage to Him. God hates divorce because it distorts the picture of His eternal commitment to us.

REFLECTIONS

God Will Justify
the Innocent

*We shall know by this that we are of the truth,
and shall assure our heart before Him,
in whatever our heart condemns us; for God is
greater than our heart, and knows all things.*

1 JOHN 3:19,20

I know there are many of you who never desired a divorce and who now feel like a second-class citizen in the family of God. Don't heap upon yourself a condemnation that is not from God. Someday those things that are hidden now will be revealed for what they are. God will justify the innocent and clear those unjustly declared guilty by man.

REFLECTIONS

Answered Prayers

*I planted, Apollos watered,
but God was causing the growth.*

1 CORINTHIANS 3:6

*W*e don't always know how our prayers will be answered, do we? I cannot tell you how often I have shared the gospel with someone sitting next to me on a plane and thought: "Their grandparents, mother, father, or wife would be so excited if only they knew how their prayers are being answered right now!"

REFLECTIONS

God Is at Work

How then shall they call upon Him in whom
they have not believed? And how shall they
believe in Him whom they have not heard?
And how shall they hear without a preacher?

ROMANS 10:14

You may not see it—but God is at work. He has a Father's heart; the world is on His heart. But He needs men and women who are established in His Word and not ashamed to share the gospel of Jesus Christ—it is the power of God unto salvation to everyone who believes, both Jew and Gentile.

REFLECTIONS

Our Time Is Short

*For who is our hope or joy or crown of
exultation? Is it not even you, in the presence
of our Lord Jesus at His coming?
For you are our glory and joy.*

1 THESSALONIANS 2:19,20

*O*ur time is short—shorter than we think. And
we can't take anything with us when this
life is over—except the souls we have invested in.

REFLECTIONS

Handling Disappointment

He knows the way I take; when He has tried me, I shall come forth as gold.

JOB 23:10

*H*ow do you handle disappointment so that you don't walk away from life thinking, "Well, it's all over now. I'll never be the same. I'll never have what I've wanted. It's gone . . . forever"? You handle it, my friend, by understanding that *disappointment is God's appointment.*

REFLECTIONS

Disappointment: A Trial of Faith

Behold, like the clay in the potter's hand,
so are you in My hand.

JEREMIAH 18:6

Disappointment is a trial of your faith. Disappointment is something which, strange as it may seem, has been filtered through God's sovereign fingers of love. He has allowed disappointment to slip through His fingers into your life, which He holds in the palm of His omnipotent hand. It has a purpose. It's for the shaping of you into a beautiful vessel of praise, honor, and glory at His coming.

REFLECTIONS

Testing Your Faith

The testing of your faith produces endurance.
And let endurance have its perfect result,
that you may be perfect and complete,
lacking in nothing.

JAMES 1:3,4

*W*hy should you consider it all joy when you encounter various trials—when you are overwhelmed with pain, captured by disappointment? Because your God commands it. And He commands it because your obedient response will be the making of you, the strengthening of your faith.

REFLECTIONS

....

....

....

....

....

Exult in Your Tribulations

We also exult in our tribulations, knowing
that tribulation brings about perseverance;
and perseverance, proven character. . . .

ROMANS 5:3,4

If the disappointment, the trial, were not
for your benefit and His glory, God would
never have permitted it. He wants you to have
every opportunity to be Christlike and fruitful.
God doesn't want you to have any regrets when
you see Him face-to-face.

REFLECTIONS

....

....

....

....

....

His Perfect Will

*The steps of a man are established by the LORD;
and He delights in his way.*

PSALM 37:23

It took more than 20 years before God revealed what He had in mind when He took Jack and me off the mission field. In my disappointment, I simply had to come to the point where I would obey His command and count it all joy—knowing He would use it to make me more like Christ and to accomplish His perfect will. (Now Precept is in more than 110 countries and 38 languages—and I stand in awe!)

REFLECTIONS

....

....

....

....

....

Enduring Heartache

The LORD is near to the brokenhearted, and
saves those who are crushed in spirit.

PSALM 34:18

Christians are not exempt from heartache, but we do have the means to endure heartache without falling apart. For this we have Jesus . . . His grace, His sufficiency. For this we have His Word . . . His promises, His wisdom.

REFLECTIONS

The Cure for Heartache

*Heal me, O LORD, and I will be healed; save
me and I will be saved, for Thou art my praise.*

JEREMIAH 17:14

I cannot change others' circumstances; I cannot cure their heartache. I cannot change my own circumstances or cure my own heartache! But I know who can. The cure for heartache is found in the Great Physician, Jehovah-rapha, and His healing balm of Gilead, the Word of God.

REFLECTIONS

Teach People the Word

Jesus therefore answered them, and said, "My teaching is not Mine, but His who sent Me."

JOHN 7:16

Teaching people the Word, showing them where to turn in the midst of their pain and confusion, helping them develop and deepen their relationship with Jesus Christ—that is what will make the difference in their difficult circumstances.

REFLECTIONS

Comforting Others

Blessed be the God and Father of our Lord
Jesus Christ, the Father of mercies and God
of all comfort; who comforts us in all our
affliction so that we may be able
to comfort those who are in any affliction
with the comfort with which we ourselves
are comforted by God.

2 CORINTHIANS 1:3,4

Our God comforts us so that we may be able, with that comfort . . . that grace . . . that strength, to comfort others. Don't waste your sorrows—help someone else.

REFLECTIONS

An Eternal Weight of Glory

*For momentary, light affliction is producing
for us an eternal weight of glory
far beyond all comparison.*

2 CORINTHIANS 4:17

Your heartaches and hurts are the very tools God will use to transform you into the image of His Son.

REFLECTIONS

An Ambassador for Christ

I have fought the good fight, I have finished the course, I have kept the faith; in the future there is laid up for me the crown of righteousness, which the Lord, the righteous Judge, will award to me on that day; and not only to me, but also to all who have loved His appearing.

2 TIMOTHY 4:7,8

You are an ambassador for Christ, pointing others away from things which are seen (the temporal) to things which are not seen (the eternal). So take courage, valiant warrior. Fight the good fight of faith, for soon it will be over and you'll be on the Victor's side, with the King you represented.

REFLECTIONS

Bear Fruit

*Truly, truly, I say to you, unless a grain of
wheat falls into the earth and dies,
it remains by itself alone; but if it dies,
it bears much fruit.*

JOHN 12:24

A crucified life cannot help but change
things . . . and people.

REFLECTIONS

August

A Shining Light

Let your light shine before men in such a
way that they may see your good works, and
glorify your Father who is in heaven.

MATTHEW 5:16

The world is looking for people who really live according to what they say they believe. What—whom—do they see in you?

REFLECTIONS

God Is Able!

LORD, who is like Thee?

PSALM 35:10

*T*oday wouldn't it be good to remember that God is able to change the hearts and minds of men and women . . . able and willing to supply all of our needs . . . able to move heaven and earth . . . able to cause all things to work together for our good and His glory? He is able!

REFLECTIONS

....

....

....

....

....

A Way of Life

*Jesus therefore answered and was saying
to them, "Truly, truly, I say to you, the Son
can do nothing of Himself, unless it is
something He sees the Father doing; for
whatever the Father does, these things the
Son also does in like manner."*

JOHN 5:19

Prayer is to be a way of life: a constant communion that causes you to commit everything to your Father for His leadership, His anointing, His provision according to His way and according to His time. Live as Jesus lived. . . .

REFLECTIONS

....

....

....

....

....

Effective Prayer

If you abide in Me, and My words
abide in you, ask whatever you wish,
and it shall be done for you.

JOHN 15:7

*E*ffective prayer, that which is born of the
Spirit, does not rip verses out of context
and fling them at the feet of God's footstool,
demanding that God come through. Effective
prayer comes when we abide in Him and His
words abide in us, and we ask according to His
will.

REFLECTIONS

....

....

....

....

He Is Waiting

Then the LORD God called to the man,
and said to him, "Where are you?"

GENESIS 3:9

Adam and Eve had just sinned. They had eaten of the forbidden fruit and were hiding from God. Yet God, who is omnipresent and omniscient, asked them where they were. God knew, but did they? Pause and take a good look at where you are, and why you're there. If you think you can hide something from God, you're wrong. Confess it. Get out in the open with God and walk with Him again in faith's obedience.

REFLECTIONS

....

....

....

....

....

The Lord Hears

*The righteous cry and the LORD hears, and
delivers them out of all their troubles.*

PSALM 34:17

I have been reading through the Old Testament for my quiet time, and I don't think I have ever been as aware as I am now of how sensitive God is to the cries of His people. How often I have reminded our Father of that lately as I have cried out to Him in my impotence. And He has not failed me. Why? Because He is the unchangeable, faithful Father who keeps His Word.

REFLECTIONS

Dependent upon God

*Then Isaiah . . . sent to Hezekiah saying,
"Thus says the LORD, the God of Israel,
'Because you have prayed to Me about
Sennacherib king of Assyria,
I have heard you.'"*

2 KINGS 19:20

O Beloved, what would happen if we prayed
more? God's ears are never closed to the
cries of His creation. When we consult God—
seeking His will, His guidance, His assistance—
we are humbling ourselves. We're saying, "God, I
am dependent upon you."

REFLECTIONS

....

....

....

....

To Him Be the Glory

*For who has known the mind of the Lord,
or who became His counselor? Or who
has first given to Him that it might be paid
back to him again? For from Him
and through Him and to Him are all things.
To Him be the glory forever. Amen.*

ROMANS 11:34-36

*W*hen we don't pray—or when our prayers
really amount to telling God what to do—
we make ourselves wiser than God by telling
Him how to direct the affairs of a universe that
He brought into existence and sustains without
any help from us. We walk in pride, saying, "I
can handle life myself."

REFLECTIONS

....

....

....

....

A Friend of the World

You adulteresses, do you not know that friendship with the world is hostility toward God? Therefore whoever wishes to be a friend of the world makes himself an enemy of God.

JAMES 4:4

Christianity never removes us from the evil world . . . it leaves us in it. But we are not to be of that world. We are not to think like the world, adapt to the world, or sell out to the world. Instead, we are to contest the world, oppose it, refuse to be conformed to it.

REFLECTIONS

....

....

....

....

....

Know the Truth

*And have mercy on some, who are doubting;
save others, snatching them out of the fire; and
on some have mercy with fear, hating even
the garment polluted by the flesh.*

JUDE 22,23

Jesus never called us to peaceful coexistence and compromise with the world and its temporary prince. Jesus leaves us here to rescue the hearts and minds of men and women and children so that they might know the truth.

REFLECTIONS

Faithful Until Death

*Be faithful until death, and I
will give you the crown of life.*

REVELATION 2:10

*W*here are the people who are willing to
seek the truth no matter what the cost?
Who are willing to risk their career, their safety,
their security, their all for the truth embodied in
our Lord Jesus Christ? Are you one such person, Beloved? A crown awaits!

REFLECTIONS

The Light of God's Word

*As a result, we are no longer to be
children . . . carried about by every wind of
doctrine, by the trickery of men . . . but
speaking the truth in love, we are to
grow up in all aspects into Him,
who is the head, even Christ.*

EPHESIANS 4:14,15

God's Word must be propagated; it must be
shared and taught. Others need to learn
how to study His Word for themselves so
that they won't be carried about by every wind
of doctrine and cunning craftiness of this evil
world. They need to know it so that they, like
you, can live in the light of it.

REFLECTIONS

....

....

....

....

....

AUGUST 13

Are You Being Threatened?

Then this Daniel began distinguishing himself among the commissioners and satraps because he possessed an extraordinary spirit. . . . Then the commissioners and satraps began trying to find a ground of accusation against Daniel. . . . But they could find no ground of accusation or evidence of corruption, inasmuch as he was faithful, and no negligence or corruption was to be found in him.

DANIEL 6:3,4

*A*re you being threatened with loss? Loss of a loved one, loss of reputation, loss of a dream, if you remain steadfast in your pursuit of the Lord and His holiness? Be a Daniel.

REFLECTIONS

....

....

....

....

....

A Steadfast Relationship with God

[Daniel] continued kneeling on his knees three
times a day, praying and giving thanks before
his God, as he had been doing previously.

DANIEL 6:10

*T*here were no starts, no stops, no interrup-
tions in Daniel's walk. Isn't that something?
Circumstances could not alter his relationship
with God. And if the powers that be didn't like
it, they would just have to feed him to the lions!
He'd rather die than compromise his God. How
about you?

REFLECTIONS

....

....

....

....

....

Facing the Lions

*Then the king gave orders, and Daniel was
brought in and cast into the lions' den.
The king spoke and said to Daniel,
"Your God whom you constantly serve
will Himself deliver you."*

DANIEL 6:16

*W*hen we face the lions we can know that,
like Daniel, we may be tossed into their
den. But we can also know that they won't
devour us. Ultimately victory will come to those
who constantly serve God, to those who won't lay
aside their communion with Him, who won't take
their eyes off Him.

REFLECTIONS

....

....

....

....

Victory Through Prayer

"Daniel, servant of the living God, has your God, whom you constantly serve, been able to deliver you from the lions?" Then Daniel spoke to the king, "O king, live forever! My God sent His angel and shut the lions' mouths, and they have not harmed me, inasmuch as I was found innocent before Him; and also toward you, O king, I have committed no crime."

DANIEL 6:20-22

Jealous men sought Daniel's demise, but Daniel came out the victor. Do victories like that just happen? No! They are won where Daniel's was—on our knees, in our closets, clinging to all that we know of our God.

REFLECTIONS

....

....

....

....

....

God's Dominion

I make a decree that in all the dominion
of my kingdom men are to fear and tremble
before the God of Daniel; for He is the living
God and enduring forever, and His kingdom is
one which will not be destroyed, and
His dominion will be forever.

DANIEL 6:26

Daniel was a man of commitment, conviction, courage, and consistency. His enemies knew it. The king knew it. His God knew it. In the end, God through Daniel brought the king to such deep conviction that King Darius issued the above decree. O that men and women would declare such things about God as a result of observing God at work in our lives.

REFLECTIONS

....

....

....

Your God Is a Lion Tamer!

Therefore, my beloved brethren, be steadfast, immovable, always abounding in the work of the Lord, knowing that your toil is not in vain in the Lord.

1 Corinthians 15:58

When your faith is challenged, when you feel threatened, remember that "by faith" Daniel "shut the mouths of lions," and you can too (Hebrews 11:33). Your God is a lion tamer!

REFLECTIONS

Our Struggle

*Our struggle is not against flesh and blood,
but against the rulers, against the powers,
against the world forces of this darkness,
against the spiritual forces of
wickedness in the heavenly places.*

EPHESIANS 6:12

Are there times when you feel as if an army has come against you? You don't know what's going to happen, but you feel it's not going to be good. What do you do? First, remember the above mentioned verse.

REFLECTIONS

The Fear You Feel

*In addition to all, taking up the shield of faith
with which you will be able to extinguish
all the flaming missiles of the evil one. . . .*

EPHESIANS 6:16

There's someone behind the fear you feel—
the enemy, that serpent of old, the devil, the
accuser of the brethren, the father of lies. What
you're imagining may or may not be fact, but either
way it's torment! Satan's fiery darts have started
fires that are hard to extinguish. But there's hope:
taking up the shield of faith . . .

REFLECTIONS

....

....

....

....

....

The Battle Is the Lord's!

The captain of the LORD'S host said
to Joshua, "Remove your sandals from
your feet, for the place where you are
standing is holy." And Joshua did so.

JOSHUA 5:15

The battle is not yours but the Lord's! And because it is His and not yours, it must be fought His way. You are to stand firm in the Lord and in the strength of His might. Deliverance comes from the Lord! Don't go into battle without the Captain of the Host.

REFLECTIONS

....

....

....

....

....

Seek the Lord

And Jehoshaphat was afraid and turned his attention to seek the LORD; and proclaimed a fast throughout all Judah.

2 CHRONICLES 20:3

*B*eloved, when you fear for your welfare . . . or when you shudder at the thought of what the future may hold . . . or when you simply hurt because others have come against you, you must do what Jehoshaphat, the king of Judah, did when he heard that a great multitude was coming against him.

REFLECTIONS

....

....

....

....

....

Trust God

*Put your trust in the LORD your God, and you
will be established. Put your trust in His
prophets [in the Word] and succeed.*

2 CHRONICLES 20:20

hough King Jehoshaphat was afraid and
didn't know what specific action to take
against the coming army, he knew where to
look. And it's the same place you, Beloved, can
look today.

REFLECTIONS

....

....

....

....

Ruler Over All

O LORD, the God of our fathers, art Thou not
God in the heavens? And art Thou not
ruler over all the kingdoms of the nations?
Power and might are in Thy hand
so that no one can stand against Thee.

2 CHRONICLES 20:6

*W*hen you feel overwhelmed because of the forces that are coming against you, remember what Jehoshaphat did (2 Chronicles 20:6-12). He focused on God, His sovereignty, His power; then he made his request according to the promises of God. This was written for your encouragement. It's an example you can follow today.

REFLECTIONS

Tell God

*They reeled and staggered like a drunken man,
and were at their wits' end. Then they cried
to the LORD in their trouble, and He
brought them out of their distresses.
He caused the storm to be still, so that the
waves of the sea were hushed. Then they
were glad because they were quiet; so He
guided them to their desired haven.*

PSALM 107:27-30

Do you feel threatened? Tell God. Cry to Him.
He is never deaf to the cry of His child.
Because you are His child and He is your Father,
your well-being is His responsibility.

REFLECTIONS

....

....

....

....

....

Talk to God

*Should evil come upon us, the sword, or
judgment, or pestilence, or famine, we will
stand . . . before Thee . . . and cry to Thee in
our distress, and Thou wilt hear and deliver
us. . . . O our God, wilt Thou not judge them?
For we are powerless before this great
multitude who are coming against us; nor do
we know what to do, but our eyes are on Thee.*

2 CHRONICLES 20:9,12

In trying times, the best thing we can do is
submit to God. Talk aloud to God. Confirm
again your desire to serve and follow Him fully.
Tell Him that your one and foremost passion is
to be found pleasing to Him.

REFLECTIONS

You're Never Alone

*Oh give us help against the adversary, for
deliverance by man is in vain. Through God
we shall do valiantly; and it is He who
will tread down our adversaries.*

PSALM 108:12,13

*R*emember, Beloved, when an adversary
comes against you, the adversary is coming
against the One who abides in you. You're never
alone, you're never without help.

REFLECTIONS

....

....

....

....

....

The Lord Will Ambush the Enemy

And when [Jehoshaphat] had consulted with the people, he appointed those who sang to the LORD and those who praised Him in holy attire, as they went out before the army and said, "Give thanks to the LORD, for His lovingkindness is everlasting."

2 CHRONICLES 20:21

Give every situation to your God. Then go forth singing His praises! The Lord will ambush the enemy. You watch. I have seen the reality of this truth many times in my own life and in the lives of others.

REFLECTIONS

True Victory

*Submit therefore to God. Resist the devil
and he will flee from you.*

JAMES 4:7

It's war! The enemy's time is short! Jesus is coming soon! But thanks be to God who always causes us to triumph in *Him*. Remember that true victory is only found in faith's obedience to God's Word. As you go forth to battle, keep bringing every thought captive to Jesus Christ and don't give the devil any place in your mind or in your life.

REFLECTIONS

The Son of the Living God

He said to them, "But who do you say that I am?" And Simon Peter answered and said, "Thou art the Christ, the Son of the living God." And Jesus answered and said to him, "Blessed are you, Simon Barjona, because flesh and blood did not reveal this to you, but My Father who is in heaven."

MATTHEW 16:15-17

God doesn't run any "Second-Hand Faith Shops."

REFLECTIONS

Your Number-One Priority

He who loves father or mother more than Me is not worthy of Me; and he who loves son or daughter more than Me is not worthy of Me.

Matthew 10:37

Never forget, Beloved, your relationship with God is your number-one priority. When you put God where He belongs, it helps you to appropriately deal with every other relationship in a freeing way—and a way pleasing to God. You may not always meet others' expectations, but you will have done what God asks—and that will bring peace to your heart and conscience.

REFLECTIONS

September

The Future Is Certain

Surely the Lord GOD does nothing
unless He reveals His secret counsel
to His servants the prophets.

AMOS 3:7

Does it seem like the world is falling apart? Do you wonder where we are headed—how it will all end? Although the future is uncertain to so many, it is not uncertain for believers. It's all recorded in the Book. God doesn't keep His children in the dark. He has a secure future for you, but you'll not be secure in it if you don't know His Book, the Bible. Knowing the Old Testament is fundamental to knowing God and understanding His plans for the future.

REFLECTIONS

·····················

Don't Be Deceived!

*And then that lawless one will be revealed whom
the Lord will slay with the breath of His mouth. . . .
That is, the one whose coming is in accord with the
activity of Satan, with all power and signs and false
wonders, and with all the deception of wickedness
for those who perish, because they did not receive
the love of the truth so as to be saved.*

2 THESSALONIANS 2:8-10

*E*vents occurring in Europe, the middle East,
and Israel are valid indicators that our Lord's
coming is near. In the last days there is going to
be a great deception and a falling away from the
faith. You must learn God's Word so that you
won't be deceived!

REFLECTIONS

·····················

·····················

·····················

·····················

·····················

Build Your Relationships

*Let love of the brethren continue. Do not
neglect to show hospitality to strangers,
for by this some have entertained angels
without knowing it. Remember
the prisoners, as though in prison with them,
and those who are ill-treated,
since you yourselves also are in the body.*

HEBREWS 13:1-3

One of the major reasons our society is falling apart is that we have neglected interpersonal relationships. We're too busy—even doing good things. Turn off the television and talk to one another. Open your home to others. Build your relationships with family and friends. Remember, people are God's utmost concern.

REFLECTIONS

....

....

....

....

Invest in the Work of God

Jesus said to him, "If you wish to be complete, go and sell your possessions and give to the poor, and you shall have treasure in heaven; and come, follow me."

MATTHEW 19:21

In light of the Lord's coming, invest in the work of God. Your treasures here are going to be destroyed, so put your money in the Lord's work, which will pay eternal dividends. Concentrate on the necessities rather than the luxuries. I know that may not be as much fun right now, but it will keep you from being ashamed when you see Him face-to-face.

REFLECTIONS

Prepare for the Days Ahead

Prepare to meet your God.

AMOS 4:12

The five words in today's Scripture have been ringing in my heart, Beloved. They are pealing from the bell tower of heaven—alerting us to the near coming of the Lord, calling us to repentance and prayer, warning us to prepare for the days ahead.

REFLECTIONS

Hate Evil; Love Good

*Seek good and not evil, that you may live; and
thus may the LORD God of hosts be with you, just
as you have said! Hate evil, love good, and establish justice in the gate! Perhaps the LORD God of
hosts may be gracious to the remnant of Joseph.*

AMOS 5:14,15

The Bible tells us that what was written beforehand in the Old Testament was written
for our learning and admonition so that through
perseverance and encouragement we might have
hope (1 Corinthians 10:11, Romans 15:4). The
prophet Amos sounds for us a call to repentance,
to prayer—a cry from the throne of God through
His prophet.

REFLECTIONS

....

....

....

....

....

It Is Not Too Late!

*For thus says the LORD to the house of Israel,
"Seek Me that you may live."*

AMOS 5:4

As God brought His judgments of locusts and fires out of control upon Israel, Amos interceded, and the Word tells us that the Lord changed His mind. It is not too late for us! Earnest prayer uttered from repentant hearts indicates God's justice when He, in mercy, spares His people.

REFLECTIONS

Never Let Go

*He also testified and said, "I have found David
the son of Jesse, a man after My heart,
who will do all My will."*

Acts 13:22

As I've prayed and read in the Psalms, I've noticed the gamut of emotions and situations David had to deal with. And I've seen how, even in his failure and sin, David never let go of God. And when David's life was over, God called him a man after His own heart!

REFLECTIONS

....

....

....

....

SEPTEMBER 9

Knowing God

*Come to Me, all who are weary and
heavy-laden, and I will give you rest.*

MATTHEW 11:28

*E*ven when I've been weak, to the place of
tears, I've found rest. Rest in the promises
of our Father, rest in the assurance that nothing
depends upon me. It all depends on Him. I'm
simply to trust and obey, to be still and know
He is God.

REFLECTIONS

....

....

....

....

....

Our Calling

Be still, and know that I am God;
I will be exalted among the nations,
I will be exalted in the earth.

PSALM 46:10 (NIV)

I couldn't do what today's Scripture calls us to if I didn't know my God and His Word. As we make knowing Him and His word our priority and passion, we will be able to rest in faith in the day of testing. And in doing so, we'll please Him—which, above all, is our calling.

REFLECTIONS

....

....

....

....

....

Do It!

*For what thanks can we render to God for you
. . . as we night and day keep praying most
earnestly that we may see your face, and may
complete what is lacking in your faith?*

1 THESSALONIANS 3:9,10

*T*here is a mandate of the church to take those
whom God saves and establish them in His
Word as that which produces reverence for Him.
Ask God who, when, and where—then do it.

REFLECTIONS

Jesus Is the Head

I am the LORD, that is My name;
I will not give My glory to another,
nor My praise to graven images.

ISAIAH 42:8

*B*eloved, don't put people on pedestals. Not one of us is sufficient in and of ourselves. Nor is any part of the body to be exalted—except the head. And Jesus is the head (Ephesians 1:22). Let's love one another, but let's not exalt anyone but Jesus.

REFLECTIONS

Led by the Spirit

Then he answered and said to me,
"This is the word of the LORD to Zerubbabel
saying, 'Not by might nor by power, but
by My Spirit,' says the LORD of hosts."

ZECHARIAH 4:6

It's time for Christians to be led by the Spirit instead of Madison Avenue. It's time for Christians to start thinking biblically and praying biblically instead of allowing themselves to be manipulated by the schemes of man. Who are we going to follow?

REFLECTIONS

....

....

....

....

....

SEPTEMBER 14

Be on the Alert

*Therefore be on the alert, for you do not know
which day your LORD is coming. . . .
For this reason you be ready too;
for the Son of Man is coming at an hour
when you do not think He will.*

MATTHEW 24:42,44

*I*t's time to serve our Lord. Pray that you'll continue to look to our precious Lord in all things. Pray that you will discern the times and be about His business while there's still time. Pray that you'll know and be established in the Word of God, living it out in a wise and uncompromising way. As you pray, pray these things for the whole body of Christ. The millennium of His coming is surely upon us.

REFLECTIONS

....

....

....

....

The Critical Difference

How blessed are those who observe His testimonies, who seek Him with all their heart.

PSALM 119:2

*W*hat difference does it make if you're not in the Word of God on a daily basis? It makes a critical difference. It's the difference between a Hi-how-are-You?-By-the-way-I've-been-meaning-to-tell-You relationship with God and a deep intimacy with your heavenly Father.

REFLECTIONS

SEPTEMBER 16

Revived Through God's Word

*This is my comfort in my affliction,
that Thy word has revived me.*

PSALM 119:50

The difference regular reading of God's Word can make in your life is the difference between a panic attack in the unexpected jolts of life and a supernatural peace in the midst of the worst storm. It's the difference between confusion and quiet confidence.

REFLECTIONS

....

....

....

....

....

In the Word

*Thy word is a lamp to my feet,
and a light to my path.*

PSALM 119:105

Does it make a difference if you're not in the Word of God on a daily basis? All the difference between a restless I-don't-know-what's-missing-but-something-is kind of feeling and a surety that all is well with your soul. It's the difference between running off in a thousand different directions and knowing that this is what you are to do.

REFLECTIONS

My Refuge

*Thou art my hiding place and my
shield; I wait for Thy word.*

PSALM 119:114

When you know God and His Word, you
know where to run for refuge, you know
where to rest your case, you know who has all
the facts. And this knowledge eases all the tension as you enter the rest of faith.

REFLECTIONS

....

....

....

....

....

SEPTEMBER 19

Food for Life

*And He humbled you and let you be hungry,
and fed you with manna . . . that He might
make you understand that man does not live by
bread alone, but man lives by everything that
proceeds out of the mouth of the LORD.*

DEUTERONOMY 8:3

If you begin to study the Bible on a daily
basis and live by what God says, you will
soon discover that being in the Word on a daily
basis is like gathering manna every day. It is food
for life. A moment with God is fine—but it's just
a nibble. I long for you to study it precept upon
precept, learning the Bible book by book.

REFLECTIONS

....

....

....

....

....

The Solution to Every Problem

If Thy law had not been my delight, then
I would have perished in my affliction.
I will never forget Thy precepts,
for by them Thou hast revived me.

PSALM 119:92,93

Do we realize that the solution to every problem, every hurt, every dilemma can be found between the covers of His holy Word—in its precepts, principles, examples, commands, promises, warnings, and teachings? To partake of it daily is to be nourished and made strong— prepared for every situation of life.

REFLECTIONS

....

....

....

....

....

Fear the Lord

> *The fear of the LORD is the*
> *beginning of knowledge.*

PROVERBS 1:7

*T*he word for "fear" in today's Scripture means a reverential trust and awesome respect. If we really respect God for who He is, then we will make listening to Him a priority. If we fear Him, we'll trust what He says and live accordingly, no matter what the situation. Then we'll have His wisdom for every situation of life.

REFLECTIONS

....

Know God

*The LORD favors those who fear Him, those
who wait for His lovingkindness.*

PSALM 147:11

When we know God through His Word and through daily intimacy with Him we retain the healthy fear (respect and trust) that God says we are to have of Him. Yet at the same time, that unhealthy dread of what God might do if we submit to Him disappears, for we know His character and comprehend the depth of His love.

REFLECTIONS

....

....

....

....

....

The Only Foundation

*The Lord GOD is my strength, and
He has made my feet like hinds' feet, and
makes me walk on my high places.*

HABAKKUK 3:19

There is no other foundation than God's Word, Beloved! No other is needed, because the Word of God is totally sufficient. If you will embrace the Word of God and bring every dilemma and lay it at the feet of God's Word, then you'll find yourself, like Habakkuk, walking with hinds' feet and not slipping.

REFLECTIONS

It Is Not Easy

*If anyone comes to Me, and does not hate
his own father and mother and wife and
children and brothers and sisters, yes, and even
his own life, he cannot be My disciple.
Whoever does not carry his own cross and
come after Me cannot be My disciple.*

LUKE 14:26,27

Have you discovered that following Jesus is not easy? Jesus never indicated that it would be. Throughout His ministry, He reminded His followers there was a cost and that they needed to count it. The rewards will come in the future.

REFLECTIONS

....

....

....

....

....

Peace in Jesus

*These things I have spoken to you, that in Me
you may have peace. In the world you
have tribulation, but take courage;
I have overcome the world.*

JOHN 16:33

O precious child of God, today will not be
without temptation, trials, testings, difficulties, and challenges. In this world we will have
tribulation. But Jesus does promise us peace—
in Him.

REFLECTIONS

....
....
....
....
....

Words of Eternal Life

Simon Peter answered Him, "Lord, to whom shall we go? You have words of eternal life."

JOHN 6:68

Only Jesus holds the words of eternal life. They're not words of death, but of life. They're not just for today, but for eternity. He knows our past, our present, our future. He's been there, and He will be there for all of our present and future circumstances.

REFLECTIONS

Words
of Truth

Sanctify them in the truth; Thy word is truth.

JOHN 17:17

*T*he words of eternal life that Jesus offers are words of truth—not lies, like the enemy's. They're the daily bread which nourishes our soul so we can confront and manage each day and all that He allows that day to bring. They set us apart and give us discernment about the issues of life that the world cannot match. We have truth—unadulterated truth.

REFLECTIONS

Where Do We Turn?

Jesus said therefore to the twelve, "You do not want to go away also, do you?" Simon Peter answered Him, "Lord, to whom shall we go? You have words of eternal life."

JOHN 6:67,68

All of us face times of incredible warfare in our lives—often on a multitude of fronts. Where do we turn? The only place to turn is to the One who has the words of eternal life!

REFLECTIONS

....

....

....

....

....

Protected by God

*I will lift up my eyes to the mountains; from
whence shall my help come? My help comes
from the LORD, who made heaven and earth.
He will not allow your foot to slip;
He who keeps you will not slumber.*

PSALM 121:1-3

*W*henever the children of Israel found
themselves in trouble, God always reminded them that He was the one who created
this world and all that is in it! If He did that—is
there anything He could not do? Of course He
could protect them! And He will protect you.

REFLECTIONS

His Throne

*Thy throne, O God, is forever and ever;
a scepter of uprightness is the
scepter of Thy kingdom.*

PSALM 45:6

*T*he sky may be absolutely black; the wind may be howling; we may be wondering if we will ever get home . . . yet we can rest in Him. God never leaves His throne.

REFLECTIONS

....

....

....

....

October

OCTOBER 1

The Promises of God

For as many as may be the promises of God, in Him they are yes; wherefore also by Him is our Amen to the glory of God through us.

2 CORINTHIANS 1:20

*W*hat do you do when you face "impossible" situations? You can decide there is no way out and run. You can be carried along by what you see, what you hear, what you're experiencing. Or you can choose the only option that comes with a warranty: run to the promises of God!

REFLECTIONS

Cling to God

"For as the waistband clings to the waist of a man, so I made the whole household of Israel and the whole household of Judah cling to Me," declares the LORD, "that they might be for Me a people, for renown, for praise, and for glory."

JEREMIAH 13:11

*W*rap yourself around God. If others entice you to doubt Him, to pull away, to let go and do it your way, don't. You'll be ruined. Cling to God no matter what and watch what you'll become.

REFLECTIONS

....

....

....

....

....

Under His Wings

*He who dwells in the shelter of the Most High
will abide in the shadow of the Almighty.
I will say to the LORD, "My refuge and my
fortress, My God, in whom I trust!"
. . . He will cover you with His pinions,
and under His wings you may seek refuge;
His faithfulness is a shield and bulwark.*

PSALM 91:1,2,4

Let's not leave the place of our appointment. There under the security of "His wings" we can dwell, knowing that whatever comes our way must first come through Him. He will be our shield.

REFLECTIONS

....

....

....

....

Trust God

*He only is my rock and my salvation, my
stronghold; I shall not be shaken.
On God my salvation and my glory rest;
the rock of my strength, my refuge is in God.
Trust in Him at all times, O people; pour out
your heart before Him; God is a refuge for us.*

PSALM 62:6-8

J don't know what disappointments you
have to face, Beloved, but I can tell you
with utmost confidence that God is no respecter of persons, only a respecter of faith.
Don't give up! Trust God's intentions and His
capabilities.

REFLECTIONS

....

....

....

....

....

The Things Above

If then you have been raised up with Christ,
keep seeking the things above. . . . Set your
mind on the things above, not on the
things that are on earth. For you have died and
your life is hidden with Christ in God.

COLOSSIANS 3:1-3

If you feel your fervor for God cooling even slightly, carefully examine your thinking and reasoning—your inner man—and carefully examine your activities—your outer man—to see if you have allowed sin to cohabit in your heart. God is a jealous God. He does not want sin in your life.

REFLECTIONS

Guard Your Heart!

*When Christ, who is our life, is revealed, then
you also will be revealed with Him in glory.
Therefore consider the members of your
earthly body as dead to immorality, impurity,
passion, evil desire, and greed, which amounts
to idolatry. For it is on account of these things
that the wrath of God will come.*

COLOSSIANS 3:4-6

Guard your heart! Immorality, wickedness,
greed, and spiritual seduction are on the
rise—and they will continue to increase.
Those who do not guard their hearts will fall
prey to these things, and the aftermath will be
bitterness of soul.

REFLECTIONS

A Way Pleasing to God

Arise, O LORD, in Thine anger; lift up Thyself
against the rage of my adversaries, and arouse
Thyself for me; Thou hast appointed judgment.
And let the assembly of the peoples encompass
Thee; and over them return Thou on high.
The LORD judges the peoples; vindicate me,
O LORD, according to my righteousness
and my integrity that is in me.

PSALM 7:6-8

*R*est assured, Beloved, the wicked will not
go unjudged. They cannot touch you
and escape His punishment. All you need to do
is make sure you behave and respond in a way
pleasing to God. Retain your integrity. He will
vindicate you.

REFLECTIONS

No Excuses

*. . . seeing that His divine power has granted
to us everything pertaining to life and
godliness, through the true knowledge of Him
who called us by His own glory and excellence.*

2 PETER 1:3

God has made every provision you need, as His child, to keep your heart pure. However, it is you responsibility to appropriate His provisions and live accordingly. No excuse will be accepted when you stand before Him!

REFLECTIONS

....

....

....

....

Watch over Your Heart

Watch over your heart with all diligence,
for from it flow the springs of life.

PROVERBS 4:23

Guard your heart so that you are steadfast, immovable, always abounding in the work of the Lord, so that you won't fall into the snare of the enemy who desires to sift you as wheat.

REFLECTIONS

....

....

....

....

....

Fear God

*The conclusion, when all has been heard, is:
fear God and keep His commandments,
because this applies to every person. For God
will bring every act to judgment, everything
which is hidden, whether it is good or evil.*

ECCLESIASTES 12:13,14

*T*here's no need to fear Satan if you'll fear
God. Watch what enters your mind. Watch
your desires. Bring every emotion to Him, and
if it's not in accord with His Word, reject it—
and you'll keep your heart pure. O Beloved,
don't put this off.

REFLECTIONS

....

....

....

....

....

OCTOBER 11

Not Just for This Life

*Not everyone who says to Me, "Lord, Lord,"
will enter the kingdom of heaven; but he who
does the will of My Father who is in heaven.*

MATTHEW 7:21

Sometimes we want Jesus Christ just for this life—as the supplier of our needs . . . the healer of our diseases . . . the provider of our necessities . . . the remover of our problems. We want Him to be liberator but not Lord. Savior but not successor to the throne. Guarantor but not guardian. Remember, He is Almighty God, deserving of our total allegiance.

REFLECTIONS

....

....

....

....

....

Peace That Brings Hope

*Let not your heart be troubled; believe in God,
believe also in Me. In my Father's house are
many dwelling places; if it were not so, I would
have told you; for I go to prepare a place for
you. And if I go and prepare a place for you, I
will come again, and receive you to Myself;
that where I am, there you may be also.*

JOHN 14:1-3

*J*esus is not just for this life. When we live
as if He is, we will be most miserable. Miserable and unable to find the deep, abiding
peace we so desperately long for—peace that
can weather any storm, peace that brings hope.

REFLECTIONS

The Prince of Peace

*These things I have spoken to you,
that in Me you may have peace. In the world
you have tribulation, but take courage;
I have overcome the world.*

JOHN 16:33

*W*here does one find peace? At the cross—no place else. Peace is found only in Christ—Christ crucified and resurrected. Christ triumphant over every pain, every sin, every failure, every disappointment, every heartbreak, every tragedy, every hope for this life. Christ . . . the Prince of peace.

REFLECTIONS

....

....

....

....

....

Life Begins at Death

Truly, truly, I [Jesus] say to you, he who hears My word, and believes Him who sent Me, has eternal life, and does not come into judgment, but has passed out of death into life.

JOHN 5:24

Either you believe what God did at Calvary and what He said and promised to those who would believe His Son, or you don't. If you believe, you will have hope—realizing that life doesn't end at death. It begins! Our brief time on earth is nothing in the light of eternity, yet we live as if it's everything.

REFLECTIONS

Hope for the Crucified

And He was saying to them all, "If anyone wishes to come after Me, let him deny himself, and take up his cross daily, and follow Me."

LUKE 9:23

*W*hen Jesus calls us to Himself for salvation, He calls us to "death"—to deny self from that day forward and to take up the cross, which is an instrument of death—Death to our desires, hopes, dreams, and ambitions by an act of the will each day. We are to choose to follow Jesus as a habit of life. It's called the crucified life by some: "Not my will but yours, Lord." Such a life brings hope for the 'crucified'—"for he who loses his life" for "His sake will save it."

REFLECTIONS

....

....

....

Look Beyond the Cost

*Jesus said, ". . . There is no one who has left
house or brothers or sisters or mother or father
or children or farms, for My sake and for the
gospel's sake, but that he shall receive a hundred
times as much now in the present age, houses
and brothers and sisters and mothers and
children and farms along with persecutions;
and in the age to come, eternal life.*

MARK 10:29,30

Let's face it, Christianity divides. It divides us
not just from the world, but many times
from loved ones—and that hurts. It hurts a whole
lot. The pain of those broken relationships, the
loss of home can be incredible. . . . Yet when and
if it comes, we must look beyond the pain to the
reward promised by Jesus Christ Himself.

REFLECTIONS

Embrace the Cross

For here we do not have a lasting city,
but we are seeking the city which is to come.

HEBREWS 13:14

*B*eloved, embrace the cross, for then your hope in Christ will move beyond this present life, and you will be of all men . . . of all women . . . most envied; for your hope will no longer be in this life, but in His life—His life in you, His life through you, and your life with Him forever.

REFLECTIONS

....

....

....

....

....

Spring Follows Winter

*Thou hast turned for me my mourning
into dancing; Thou hast loosed my
sackcloth and girded me with gladness.*

PSALM 30:11

here is hope at the cross. Weeping endures
for a night—so weep, but know that joy does
come in the morning. Spring follows winter.
Resurrection follows death. He promised and
He cannot lie.

REFLECTIONS

....

....

....

....

OCTOBER 19

Before the Throne of God

Worthy art Thou, our Lord and our God,
to receive glory and honor and power.

REVELATION 4:11

Don't you want your life to be an expression of the truth that Jesus Christ is worthy of honor, of glory, of blessing? To demonstrate His worthiness? One day, Beloved, Revelation 4:11 will be our song as we join others from every tribe and tongue and people and nation before the throne of God! Start practicing now!

REFLECTIONS

....

....

....

....

....

A Glimpse into the Future

Worthy is the Lamb that was slain to receive
power and riches and wisdom and might
and honor and glory and blessing.

REVELATION 5:12

In Revelation 4 and 5 God gives us a dramatic, graphic glimpse into the future and the glory that will be given to our Redeemer. You and I need to recognize and live in a way that testifies that Jesus is worthy to receive power and riches and wisdom and might and honor and glory and blessing now in the everyday affairs of our lives!

REFLECTIONS

....

....

....

....

....

Who Brought You There?

*And when you were dead in your
transgressions and the uncircumcision of your
flesh, He made you alive together with Him,
having forgiven us all our transgressions,
having canceled out the certificate of debt
consisting of decrees against us and which was
hostile to us; and He has taken it out of the
way, having nailed it to the cross.*

COLOSSIANS 2:13,14

*H*ow does your life express the worthiness
of the One who conquered sin and death
by redeeming you with His own blood? Who
paid the penalty for all your sins? Who removed
your sins as far as from the east to the west? Are
you living worthily of the One who brought you
to Himself at such a cost?

REFLECTIONS

....

....

....

Some Practical Questions

Therefore be imitators of God, as beloved children; and walk in love, just as Christ also loved you, and gave Himself up for us, an offering and a sacrifice to God as a fragrant aroma.

EPHESIANS 5:1,2

*B*eloved, examine your life in the light of His worthiness and ask yourself some very practical questions: Does the way you use your abilities, your energies show His pre-eminence in your life? Is the wisdom that you absorb and proclaim worthy of the Lord? Does your life honor who He is?

REFLECTIONS

....

....

....

....

God Is I Am

*And God said to Moses, "I AM WHO I AM.
. . . This is My name forever, and this is
My memorial-name to all generations."*

EXODUS 3:14,15

*A*re you dealing with fear? Fear not, Beloved, because your God is I AM. He is everything and anything you'll ever need. I AM is His memorial name to all generations—even to ours (Exodus 3:14,15). God is never anything less than He has been in the past, and He never moves from His throne. He is in charge, and He is there for you.

REFLECTIONS

Rest, Beloved

Return to your rest, O my soul, for the
LORD has dealt bountifully with you.

PSALM 116:7

*R*est—cease striving, Beloved. Bury your
head in His all-sufficient breast. Call
upon your El Shaddai, your all-sufficient Father.
He says, *"Do not be afraid; I am the first and the*
last" (Revelation 1:17). He's there before the
fear comes, and He will be there when it's all
over—ever the same, never changed or altered
by time or man.

REFLECTIONS

You Are Precious

*Are not two sparrows sold for a cent? And yet
not one of them will fall to the ground apart
from your Father. But the very hairs of your
head are all numbered. Therefore do not fear;
you are of more value than many sparrows.*

MATTHEW 10:29-31

*R*emember you are of great value, great
worth to God. Whether you believe it or
not, you are precious to Him. He created you
out of His good pleasure for it pleased God to
bring you into existence. It didn't matter whether
any person wanted you or not—God did. This is
why you exist. So hold your head high, dear child
of God, for you are precious in His sight.

REFLECTIONS

The Son Never Ceases to Shine

I sought the LORD, and He answered me,
and delivered me from all my fears.
They looked to Him and were radiant, and
their faces shall never be ashamed.
This poor man cried and the LORD heard him,
and saved him out of all his troubles.

PSALM 34:4-6

When all seems dark, remember the Son never ceases to shine. Look to Him. Cry to Him. He will dispel the darkness of the blackest night.

REFLECTIONS

....

....

....

....

....

Find Refuge in God

When my anxious thoughts multiply within me, Thy consolations delight my soul.

PSALM 94:19

*W*hat can you do when fear strikes? Get into the Word of God. If you don't know where to turn in the Word and if God doesn't lay any specific passages on your heart, turn to the Psalms. Find refuge in God and His infallible Word. Read until His peace mounts a guard around your mind, heart, and soul.

REFLECTIONS

Fear Not

Do not fear, for I am with you;
do not anxiously look about you, for I am your
God. I will strengthen you, surely I will
help you, surely I will uphold you
with My righteous right hand.

ISAIAH 41:10

*F*ear not, little sheep. Your Shepherd is there, Someday when you turn around you'll see, as Psalm 23:6 says, goodness and mercy really were following you all the days of your life.

REFLECTIONS

It Works!

He caused the storm to be still, so that the
waves of the sea were hushed. Then they were
glad because they were quiet; so He guided
them to their desired haven.

Psalm 107:29,30

*W*hen you know Jesus—when you understand that Jesus is not only Creator but Sustainer of all that exists in heaven and earth— you can be at peace even in the storm. You can quit struggling and rest in His sovereignty over the storm-tossed waves of life. He's God over the raging seas, the tumultuous circumstances. So let Him hush the storm and quiet your heart. When God speaks, it is as good as done.

REFLECTIONS

Counseling Others

As the LORD lives, what my God says,
that I will speak.

2 CHRONICLES 18:13

Have you ever counseled another Christian and told him or her how to handle his or her situation? If you ever advise another, make sure you are giving instruction that is in accordance with the whole counsel of God's Word. If you give counsel that contradicts God's Word, you could cause other people to turn aside from God's will for their lives (see Malachi 2:8,9).

REFLECTIONS

....

....

....

....

....

In Line with God's Word

*If they speak not according to this
word, it is because there is no light in them.*

ISAIAH 8:20 (KJV)

Since God's Word advises *"let not many of you
become teachers . . . knowing that as such we
shall incur a stricter judgment"* (James 3:1), does
that mean that it is wrong for one Christian to
seek counsel from another? No, counsel is fine
as long as it is in line with God's Word. Just
remember the counselor, the teacher, carries a
weighty responsibility.

REFLECTIONS

....

....

....

....

....

November

A Steadfast Confidence

*For this reason I also suffer these things,
but I am not ashamed; for I know whom
I have believed and I am convinced that
He is able to guard what I have
entrusted to Him until that day.*

2 TIMOTHY 1:12

Yes, Beloved, a life of intimacy with God requires discipline, but it will give you a steadfast confidence through the most difficult of trials.

REFLECTIONS

....

....

....

....

....

Intimacy with God

But godliness actually is a means of great gain,
when accompanied by contentment. . . .
And if we have food and covering,
with these we shall be content.

1 TIMOTHY 6:6,8

*W*e're responsible to work, to earn our living. However, if you want to pursue intimacy with God you may have to be satisfied with less, rather than working harder and longer hours in order to have more. How awful it would be to accumulate the world's treasure and accolades and miss knowing God intimately.

REFLECTIONS

....

....

....

....

....

How Do You Seek God?

*The sum of Thy word is truth, and every one of
Thy righteous ordinances is everlasting.*

PSALM 119:160

How do you seek God? You begin by being
in His Word consistently. Three minutes
a day isn't going to do it if you're going to know
the whole counsel of God! Get one of the
International Inductive Study Series* and do it.
It will take you by the hand and lead you
through the Word day by day. You'll be awed at
what you learn and how it will deepen your
relationship with and understanding of God.

*Harvest House Publishers, written by Kay Arthur.

REFLECTIONS

NOVEMBER 4

Forgiveness

*For if while we were enemies, we were
reconciled to God through the death of
His Son, much more, having been
reconciled, we shall be saved by His life.*

ROMANS 5:10

*F*orgiveness! How we all need it. God came
into the world in the form of man to reconcile us to Himself (Hebrews 2:9,14). But there
could be no reconciliation until His Son, who
knew no sin, was made sin for us (2 Corinthians
5:21). The manger was shadowed with a cross!
Jesus was born to die so that you and I, who in
no way deserve it, might have forgiveness of sins.

REFLECTIONS

....

....

....

....

Our Sins

*Father, forgive them; for they do
not know what they are doing.*

LUKE 23:34

*O*ur sins were the nails that held Jesus on
Calvary's tree.

REFLECTIONS

....

....

....

....

....

NOVEMBER 6

Forgive and Be Forgiven

*For if you forgive men for their transgressions,
your heavenly Father will also forgive you.
But if you do not forgive men, then your
Father will not forgive your transgressions.*

MATTHEW 6:14,15

If Jesus is willing to forgive us when it was our sins that caused His death, and if God the Father is willing to forgive, can we, who have so grievously sinned against Him, withhold forgiveness?

REFLECTIONS

Total Forgiveness

[We are] justified as a gift by His grace through
the redemption which is in Christ Jesus.

ROMANS 3:24

Hope, peace, and strength are found at His cross, where you have received absolute and total forgiveness for all your sins—past, present, and future. If you have no peace because of your sins, no hope because of what you did in the past, if you think you cannot go on—there is only one place you can change all that, and it's at the cross of Jesus Christ.

REFLECTIONS

NOVEMBER 8

By the Grace
of God

*This is the only thing I want to find out from
you: did you receive the Spirit by the works of
the Law, or by hearing with faith? Are you so
foolish? Having begun by the Spirit, are you
now being perfected by the flesh?*

GALATIANS 3:2,3

If it took grace to save us, how can we think
that it takes our own skill to make it in the
Christian life? If our own efforts and merit
couldn't take care of our sin and failure in the
first place, what makes you think they can now?

REFLECTIONS

....

....

....

....

....

NOVEMBER 9

God Cannot Lie

*And they overcame him because of the
blood of the Lamb and because of the
word of their testimony, and they did
not love their life even to death.*

REVELATION 12:11

The devil is having a heyday among Christians today because, through one means or another, he's blinding them to who they are in Christ. Satan is feeding them a lie, and they're swallowing the bait—hook, line, and sinker. Has it happened to you, Beloved? Remember that God cannot lie, and He says you are in Him and He is in you. You couldn't be more secure.

REFLECTIONS

NOVEMBER 10

The Great Shepherd

*Now the God of peace, who brought up from
the dead the great Shepherd of the sheep
through the blood of the eternal covenant,
even Jesus our Lord, equip you in every good
thing to do His will, working in us that which
is pleasing in His sight, through Jesus Christ,
to whom be the glory forever and ever. Amen.*

HEBREWS 13:20,21

*W*hen sheep become tense, edgy, and restless, the shepherd will quietly move
through the flock, and his very presence will release the tension of the sheep and quiet their
anxieties. Their shepherd is there!

REFLECTIONS

My Only Desire

*With Thy counsel Thou wilt guide me,
and afterward receive me to glory.*

PSALM 73:24

Jesus Christ alone is to be my one desire—His life, not mine. I am to love Him above all else, above all others. And if choices are to be made, I must choose Him. Let Psalm 73:24 be your heart's cry.

REFLECTIONS

....

....

....

....

....

NOVEMBER 12

From the Heart

*But the things that proceed out of the
mouth come from the heart, and those defile
the man. For out of the heart come evil
thoughts, murders, adulteries, fornications,
thefts, false witness, slanders. These are
the things which defile the man.*

MATTHEW 15:18-20

Our tendency is to spend all our time worrying
about how we look on the outside. But God
tells us to watch over our heart (mind) with all
diligence, for it is what comes from the heart
that defiles us.

REFLECTIONS

....

....

....

....

....

NOVEMBER 13

God Is on His Throne

But the LORD is in His holy temple. Let all the earth be silent before Him. . . . For the earth will be filled with the knowledge of the glory of the LORD, as the waters cover the sea.

HABAKKUK 2:20,14

The world may worship idols, justice may be perverted, wickedness may surround us; strife, destruction, and violence may be the order of the day, but God is still on His throne.

REFLECTIONS

....

....

....

....

NOVEMBER 14

The Fullness of Redemption

Behold, the tabernacle of God is among men, and He shall dwell among them, and they shall be His people, and God Himself shall be among them, and He shall wipe away every tear from their eyes. . . . The first things have passed away.

REVELATION 21:3,4

Could you do with a little joy? Do you wish for the quiet and sure confidence of a future that is not the fruit of your yesterdays? Don't faint, precious child of God. Your day of jubilee is coming. The fullness of your redemption is yet to be experienced!

REFLECTIONS

The Year of Jubilee

You shall thus consecrate the fiftieth year. . . .
It shall be a jubilee for you, and each of
you shall return to his own property,
and each of you shall return to his
family. . . . He who overcomes shall
inherit these things, and I will be his
God and he will be My son.

LEVITICUS 25:10; REVELATION 21:7

Leviticus 25 describes the year of jubilee. Every 50 years those who had been sold into slavery could return home, and those who had lost land they once owned would have it returned. Imagine the hope this would bring! No wonder God called it a year of jubilee! What a jubilee awaits us when we regain what Adam lost—dominion with Christ over the world.

REFLECTIONS

....

....

....

Don't Write God Off

*And I say to you, ask, and it shall be given
to you; seek, and you shall find;
knock, and it shall be opened to you.*

LUKE 11:9

*A*re you agonizing in prayer for someone or something, and God hasn't answered? Are you about to quit? O Beloved, don't write God off. Don't lose hope. In today's verse Jesus tells us to keep on keeping on. Ask, seek, and knock are all present tense verbs here in the original Greek. They speak of *continuous* or *habitual* action.

REFLECTIONS

Persistence

*I tell you, even though he will not get up and
give him anything because he is his friend,
yet because of his persistence he will
get up and give him as much as he needs.*

LUKE 11:8

One of the major keys to answered prayer is
persistence. After giving the disciples what
we call "The Lord's Prayer," Jesus posed the
question about going to a friend's house at midnight for a loaf of bread. Do you remember what
Jesus said about the friend?

REFLECTIONS

God Has a Purpose

*Now He was telling them a parable
to show that at all times they
ought to pray and not to lose heart.*

LUKE 18:1

Persist! It's more tempting to quit praying than to persist, isn't it? . . . More tempting to throw up our hands in defeat than to hold on in faith? We're so impatient. But when we get impatient and do it our way, we mess up. If there's a delay in the answer, Beloved, you can be sure it's because God has a purpose.

REFLECTIONS

Prayer Opens Doors

*. . . praying at the same time for us as well,
that God may open up to us a door
for the word, so that we may speak
forth the mystery of Christ.*

COLOSSIANS 4:3

For 40 years Bill Bright prayed every single day, asking God to open Russia for the gospel. He never stopped. The discouraging news about Russia under Communist rule never hindered Bill's prayers. Then the Iron Curtain came down. After 40 years of prayer, Bill was given the awesome opportunity to preach to thousands in Moscow. He won it on his knees.

REFLECTIONS

....

....

....

....

The Son Sets You Free

*If therefore the Son shall make
you free, you shall be free indeed.*

JOHN 8:36

For years Jack and I cried out to God for our oldest son, Tom. I did all I could to turn him around. Finally in 1991 God said, "Be still, Kay, and know that I am God." I was now to be quiet—no more talking, persuading, pleading, debating. I was shut up to nothing but trusting God. To be still means to cease striving. What intimacy this brings—what utter dependence. Then, in 1992, God did what only God can do— He set our 37-year-old son free. And my, how he loves our Lord and His Word!

REFLECTIONS

....

....

....

....

NOVEMBER 21

Only God Can

Trust in the LORD with all your heart,
and do not lean on your own understanding.
In all your ways acknowledge Him,
and He will make your paths straight.

PROVERBS 3:5,6

Try as we might, we cannot change another person's heart. Only God can. God alone is our hope, our very present hope in the time of need and trouble. When will we learn to simply do what God says:

- to pray and not faint,
- to persist and not quit,
- to wait upon Him until He brings it to pass?

REFLECTIONS

It Will Come

*[It is God] who does great things,
unfathomable, and wondrous
works without number.*

JOB 9:10

If you're convinced by God's Spirit that what you're asking for is in accord with God's Word, His will, and His character, and you're not asking merely to satisfy your own desires (James 4:2,3), then persist. Though the answer to your prayer tarries—even for years—it will come.

REFLECTIONS

The Wrong Way Out

*Blessed is a man who perseveres under trial;
for once he has been approved, he will
receive the crown of life, which the Lord
has promised to those who love Him.*

JAMES 1:12

*H*ave you ever wanted to take the wrong way out? To let your emotions and thoughts run amuck, rather than allowing the Spirit of God to help you keep them under His control? I understand—I've been there. Listen to His words in James 1:12.

REFLECTIONS

....

....

....

....

....

The World's Mold

*And do not be conformed to this world, but be
transformed by the renewing of your mind,
that you may prove what the will of God is,
that which is good and acceptable and perfect.*

ROMANS 12:2

*B*eloved, have you noticed how much of the
world's philosophies have been integrated
into the church's worship, counsel, thinking, and
teaching? If we have a steady diet of these things
and neglect the Bible itself, is it any wonder that
the world has squeezed us into its mold—and
that we can barely recognize it?

REFLECTIONS

Beware

*Beware, and be on your guard against
every form of greed; for not even when
one has an abundance does his life
consist of his possessions.*

LUKE 12:15

For the next few days let me give you a sampling of where we are off truth's center if we embrace the world's philosophies. Sometimes we think: "Things will make me happy," but God's Word warns against this.

REFLECTIONS

....

....

....

....

....

A Close-Knit Family
or Divided?

*Do you suppose that I came to grant peace on
earth? I tell you, no, but rather division;
for from now on five members in one
household will be divided, three
against two, and two against three.*

LUKE 12:51,52

Sometimes we think: A close-knit, happy family is evidence that I am blessed of God and have raised my children properly. But this is not always true. Listen to what Jesus said in Luke 12:51,52.

REFLECTIONS

My First Obligation

*Truly I say to you, there is no one who has
left house or wife or brothers or parents or
children, for the sake of the kingdom of God,
who shall not receive many times as much at
this time and in the age to come, eternal life.*

LUKE 18:29,30

Sometimes we think: I can't do that for the
Lord; my first obligation is to my family. Be
careful, Beloved, that you don't put family above
God.

REFLECTIONS

....

....

....

....

....

NOVEMBER 28

You May Be Tested

*I know your tribulation and your poverty
(but you are rich), and the blasphemy
by those who say they are Jews and are not,
but are a synagogue of Satan. Do not fear what
you are about to suffer. Behold, the devil is
about to cast some of you into prison,
that you may be tested, and you will have
tribulation ten days. Be faithful until death,
and I will give you the crown of life.*

REVELATION 2:9,10

Sometimes we think: If I have enough faith,
or speak words of faith, I'll not suffer, I'll
always prosper. Read what God's Word says
in Revelation 2:9,10.

REFLECTIONS

Promotion Comes from God

For it is written, "I will destroy the wisdom of the wise, and the cleverness of the clever I will set aside." Where is the wise man? Where is the scribe? Where is the debater of this age? Has not God made foolish the wisdom of the world?

1 CORINTHIANS 1:19,20

Our thinking says: If our kids are going to make it in this world, they've got to be educated by the world. Yet promotion comes from God.

REFLECTIONS

NOVEMBER 30

Your Bread
of Life

*But He answered and said, "It is written, 'Man
shall not live on bread alone, but on every
word that proceeds out of the mouth of God'."*

MATTHEW 4:4

Esteem God's Word as more precious than
your necessary food—because it is. It is your
bread of life . . . it is the light for your path
. . . it is the place where you can rest in peace
and contentment.

REFLECTIONS

....

....

....

....

....

December

Do Decembers Fragment You?

No soldier in active service entangles himself in the affairs of everyday life, so that he may please the one who enlisted him as a soldier.

2 TIMOTHY 2:4

How I love the holidays that are upon us, and how I delight in fixing up the house for family and friends! Yet, I have to watch myself that I don't get so busy, so involved in the social occasions, so fragmented, and so worn out that I miss the spiritual blessing of Christmas.

Determine that you are going to begin each day of this month quietly before the Lord, reading a chapter a day of the Gospel of Matthew, asking God to speak to you in special ways. There are 28 chapters, so on December 24 and 25 read Luke 1 and 2, and then resume with Matthew 24 and finish out the month. Watch the difference doing this will make in your Christmas.

Ashamed of Your Past?

*And to Salmon was born Boaz by Rahab; and
to Boaz was born Obed by Ruth; and to Obed,
Jesse; and to Jesse was born David the king.
And to David was born Solomon by her who
had been the wife of Uriah.*

MATTHEW 1:5,6

Sometimes we feel like we don't have a
chance because of our genealogy—or our
past. Put away those feelings. Look who's
mentioned in the genealogy of our Lord! A harlot
by the name of Rahab, who believed God and
was rescued from death. A Gentile by the name
of Ruth, a woman who was an outsider because
she wasn't an Israelite. And finally, a woman who
had an adulterous affair and bore another man's
son. Her name was Bathsheba, the wife of Uriah.

Interesting, isn't it, that God chose to mention
only these three women's names and that of
Mary, a woman who kept herself pure. You know
God had a purpose—to give you and me hope,
Beloved.

"How Are You Really Doing?"

Beloved, let us love one another, for love is from God; and everyone who loves is born of God and knows God. . . . Bear one another's burdens, and thus fulfill the law of Christ.

1 JOHN 4:7; GALATIANS 6:2

Time and distance keep us from doing this, but if it were possible, I would love to knock on your front door and have you invite me in for a cup of coffee and a chat. If we could just get past the "Hi! How are you?" I would want to know, "How are you doing . . . really doing?" It helps to talk to a person who will bear your burdens and seek God's wisdom for you in your life.

REFLECTIONS

....

....

....

....

DECEMBER 4

All the Answers

*Establish Thy word to Thy servant, as that
which produces reverence for Thee. . . .
May Thy compassion come to me that I may
live, for Thy law is my delight.*

PSALM 119:38,77

I wish I could share with you some of the
letters I receive. Like me, you'd be heart-
broken over the pain many have and are enduring.
But you would also be so awed and encouraged
at what God does when individuals decide to
believe Him. The Word of God has the answers.
It is the answer to every circumstance of life.

REFLECTIONS

....

....

....

....

....

DECEMBER 5

Rest in God's Presence

Blessed is the man who trusts in the LORD
and whose trust is the LORD. For he will be
like a tree planted by the water, that extends its
roots by a stream and will not fear when
the heat comes; but its leaves will be green,
and it will not be anxious in a year of
drought nor cease to yield fruit.

JEREMIAH 17:7,8

*R*est, dear one, in His presence, in His promises. God, and God alone, holds your life and well-being in His loving and kind hands.

REFLECTIONS

....

....

....

....

....

DECEMBER 6

God Knows

*Come to Me, all who are weary and
heavy-laden, and I will give you rest.
Take My yoke upon you, and learn from Me,
for I am gentle and humble in heart;
and you shall find rest for your souls.
For My yoke is easy, and My load is light.*

MATTHEW 11:28-30

How are you doing on the inside where others cannot see—or are not allowed? Are you scared, troubled, wondering about your job? Your health? How you are going to care for your parents? Whatever your situation, God knows exactly where you are, what you are going through, and what your future holds.

REFLECTIONS

....

....

....

....

....

DECEMBER 7

The Lord
Who Is There

*For I, the LORD, do not change. . . . Every good thing
bestowed and every perfect gift is from above,
coming down from the Father of lights, with whom
there is no variation, or shifting shadow.*

MALACHI 3:6; JAMES 1:17

God, the omnipotent One, is always there.
He always has the answers. Nothing—no
one—can ever drive Him away. Your personality, your behavior, your response will never
alter who He is or what He has promised. He is
God; He cannot change. His name is *Jehovah-
Shammah*, the Lord who is there.

REFLECTIONS

Who's in Charge?

*I glorified Thee on the earth, having
accomplished the work which
Thou hast given Me to do.*

JOHN 17:4

*A*re others trying to run your life? Are you
trying to please men? Who's in charge? Is
not God our director—and our audience? Like
Jesus, you only have to please your Father. Like
Jesus, you want to say: *I glorified thee on the
earth. . . .*

REFLECTIONS

The Battle Must Be Won

Teach me Thy way, O LORD: I will walk in Thy truth; unite my heart to fear Thy name.
I will give thanks to Thee, O Lord my God, with all my heart, and will glorify Thy name forever.

PSALM 86:11,12

There's so much noise—so many people pulling on us—that being alone and quiet before the Lord can be a battle. But if, like Jesus, you want to be able to say that you have glorified God on earth and finished the work He's given you to do, the battle must be won.

REFLECTIONS

....

Cry Out to God!

[Say with Shadrach, Meshach and Abednego:]
"If it be so, our God whom we serve is able
to deliver us from the furnace of blazing fire;
and He will deliver us out of your hand,
O king. But even if He does not, let it be
known to you, O king, that we are not
going to serve your gods or worship the
golden image that you have set up."

DANIEL 3:17,18

There are times when we must take a stand rather than bow in submission to something that just isn't right or pleasing to God. And when we can't bend or bow, we must be willing—like Shadrach, Meshach and Abendnego—to suffer the consequences. God is able to deliver and may—but if not, know He has a higher purpose. He'll walk into the furnace with us and never leave us alone in the fire.

....

....

Lay Hold of God

The Lord is my helper, I will not be afraid.
What shall man do to me?

HEBREWS 13:6

*F*lee to God's refuge by laying hold of the hope set before you. Remember, your heavenly Father is there, arms open wide. Come to Him as a child would. Dwell between His shoulders. He is Abba—your Father God.

REFLECTIONS

....

....

....

....

....

God's Cornerstone

*Behold I lay in Zion a choice stone, a
precious cornerstone, and he who believes
in Him shall not be disappointed.*

1 PETER 2:6

Find a stone—one big enough to write on.
Then with a permanent marking pen, write
EBENEZER on it and say with Samuel: *"Thus
far the Lord has helped us"* (1 Samuel 7:12).
Ebenezer means "the stone of help." Then,
when you look at your stone, remember God's
cornerstone, the Lord Jesus Christ, the foundation stone that God laid in Zion almost 2,000
years ago.

REFLECTIONS

DECEMBER 13

"Keep On Keeping On"

*Be strong and very courageous. . . . Do not turn . . .
to the right or to the left. . . . This book of the law
shall not depart from your mouth, but you shall
meditate on it day and night, so that you may be
careful to do according to all that is written in it;
for then you will make your way prosperous.*

JOSHUA 1:7,8

Although the child of God is not to be overcome by circumstances, not to be embittered with God, nor to lose hope, sometimes it is
difficult to "keep on keeping on," isn't it? How can
we? Conquering life seems overwhelming and,
like Joshua, we feel so impotent. What does God
say?

REFLECTIONS

....

....

....

....

....

Go Forward

*But Jesus said to him, "No one, after putting
his hand to the plow and looking back,
is fit for the kingdom of God."*

LUKE 9:62

To be a courageous child of our loving Father
you must go forward in the path He has set
before you.

REFLECTIONS

....

....

....

....

....

DECEMBER 15

Go Forward in Faith

*These things I have spoken to you, that in
Me you may have peace. In the world
you have tribulation, but take courage;
I have overcome the world.*

JOHN 16:33

*T*o be courageous is to face difficulty or danger in the confidence that God will bring His perfect will to pass. You are to believe and go forward in faith. You're not alone for He is with you. Listen to our Lord's promise to His disciples in John 16:33, and then memorize Hebrews 13:5,6. It will be well worth it, my friend.

REFLECTIONS

....

....

....

....

....

DECEMBER 16

He Gives Strength

*He gives strength to the weary, and to him
who lacks might He increases power.*

ISAIAH 40:29

*B*eloved, do you find yourself saying: "How
can I be strong and courageous when I feel
ordinary, unimportant, and weak?" Remember
what He gives and to whom. When you are
weak, then you're strong because you're appro-
priating what's yours in Him.

REFLECTIONS

....

....

....

....

DECEMBER 17

Obedience and Faith

You shall therefore keep every commandment
which I am commanding you today,
so that you may be strong and go in and possess
the land into which you are about to cross.

DEUTERONOMY 11:8

Loving obedience makes you strong. Faith—
believing God's Word and standing on it—
makes you courageous.

REFLECTIONS

Is There a Void in Your Life?

*And my God shall supply all your needs
according to His riches in glory in Christ Jesus.*

PHILIPPIANS 4:19

Is there a void in your life? Then what you need is a Merry Christmas! You need the relationship that Christmas is all about. You need Jesus, God in the flesh, who gives you access to the Father. You need a Father who not only promises to supply all your needs through His Son, but One who is capable and willing to do so.

REFLECTIONS

....

....

....

....

....

The Angels Sang!

*And suddenly there appeared with the angel
a multitude of the heavenly host praising
God, and saying, "Glory to God in the
highest, and on earth peace among
men with whom He is pleased."*

LUKE 2:13,14

*E*very December for almost 2,000 years men
and women have looked back incredulously
to the day that saw a 4,000-year-old prophecy
fulfilled as God came forth from Mary's womb.
Ordained the Lamb that would take away the
sins of the world, there He was—God, clothed
with the flesh of mankind. No wonder the angels
sang!

REFLECTIONS

Don't Miss It!

*From the offspring of this man [David],
according to promise, God has brought to Israel
a Savior Jesus. . . . Those who live in Jerusalem,
and their rulers, recognize neither Him nor the
utterances of the prophets which are read every
Sabbath, fulfilled these by condemning Him.*

ACTS 13:23,27

*B*efore mankind's very eyes, 333 prophecies were
fulfilled in Jesus' first coming, one by one until
after 33 years the Christ—Messiah—died and rose
again. They shouldn't have missed what was
happening. And neither should we! For He was the
Promised One, the only giver of eternal Life.

REFLECTIONS

Wonderful Counselor

For a child will be born to us, a son will be given to us; and the government will rest on His shoulders; and His name will be called Wonderful Counselor. . . .

ISAIAH 9:6

Do you know what God did when He gave you Jesus? He put the government of your life on His shoulders. Whatever your situation, you now have Jesus as your *Wonderful Counselor*. Are you running to Him for help? Don't run anywhere else unless your Wonderful Counselor tells you to, and check out all you hear with His written Word.

REFLECTIONS

Mighty God

*The government will rest on His
shoulders; and His name will be called
Wonderful Counselor, Mighty God. . . .*

ISAIAH 9:6

Jesus is filtering every aspect of your life through His omnipotent fingers of love. All that comes into your life will eventually work together for your good and His glory. It will be used to make you like Him, and on that day when you see Him face-to-face, you will have no regrets.

REFLECTIONS

....

....

....

....

....

Eternal Father

*The government will rest on His shoulders;
and His name will be called Wonderful
Counselor, Mighty God, Eternal Father. . . .*

ISAIAH 9:6

*R*emember, Beloved, you have an *Eternal Father*. You can snuggle in His all-sufficient arms. He is never too busy, never plays favorites with His other children, and is always impartial. If you want to be mightily used by Him in His kingdom, He will see that it happens . . . as you listen to Him, obey Him, and serve Him with singleness of heart.

REFLECTIONS

Prince of Peace

His name will be called Wonderful Counselor,
Mighty God, Eternal Father, Prince of Peace.

ISAIAH 9:6

Sin alienates us from God and puts us at enmity with Him. It makes us enemies of God. And until the issue of sin is dealt with and paid in full, there can be no reconciliation. Thus God moved on our behalf. He sent the only One who can reconcile us to Himself—the Prince of Peace, the Lord Jesus Christ—by paying for all our sins.

This is what Christmas is all about, Beloved—peace with God through the birth, death, and resurrection of our Lord Jesus. If you have believed—or will believe—that Jesus Christ is God, your substitute for your sins and your savior, then you will know and have the Prince of Peace.

DECEMBER 25

God's Christmas Tree

*But as many as received Him, to them He gave
the right to become children of God, even
to those who believe in His name.*

JOHN 1:12

God's Christmas tree is the cross. This is where God hung His gift—His only begotten Son—for you. Have you, my friend, received God's gift or is it still sitting there, unopened? Don't open man's gifts and miss the gift of eternal life. Today is the day of salvation.

REFLECTIONS

....

....

....

....

....

DECEMBER 26

The People of God

*But you are a chosen race, a royal priesthood,
a holy nation, a people for God's own posses-
sion, that you may proclaim the excellencies
of Him who has called you out of darkness
into His marvelous light; for you once were
not a people, but now you are the people of
God; you had not received mercy, but
now you have received mercy.*

1 PETER 2:9,10

God calls us the "people of God." Think of
what this means, Beloved! You belong! You
belong to God Almighty! Raise that head
that hangs down, put those shoulders back,
o child of the King! Your sins are forgiven.
You're part of a royal priesthood . . . chosen by
God. Now live accordingly.

REFLECTIONS

Accept Forgiveness

*Thou, in Thy great compassion, didst not
forsake them in the wilderness; the
pillar of cloud did not leave them by day,
to guide them on their way, nor the pillar
of fire by night, to light for them the
way in which they were to go. . . .
The joy of the LORD is your strength.*

NEHEMIAH 9:19; 8:10

Do you weep when you hear God's Word and
think of how greatly you failed Him in the
past? Weep for the sin of unbelief. Have a godly
sorrow, but don't keep weeping, for that is unbelief. Salvation is a new beginning. It is a new
power—the power of the indwelling Holy
Spirit, who will never leave you but who will
guide you into a life of righteousness. So accept
His forgiveness and go forward as a new creature in Christ Jesus.

The Gift of Eternal Life

*Grace and peace be multiplied to you in the
knowledge of God and of Jesus our Lord; seeing that His divine power has granted to us
everything pertaining to life and godliness,
through the true knowledge of Him who
called us by His own glory and excellence.*

2 PETER 1:2,3

If you have received the gift of eternal life
by genuinely putting your trust in Jesus
Christ, then you've experienced His grace and
His peace. But don't stop there. Let . . . *grace
and peace be multiplied to you in the knowledge
of God and of Jesus our Lord. . . .*

REFLECTIONS

DECEMBER 29

Don't Stagnate

Applying all diligence, in your faith supply moral excellence, and in your moral excellence, knowledge; and in your knowledge, self-control, and in your self-control, perseverance, and in your perseverance, godliness; and in your godliness, brotherly kindness, and in your brotherly kindness, love. For if these qualities are yours and are increasing, they render you neither useless nor unfruitful in the true knowledge of our Lord Jesus Christ.

2 PETER 1:5-8

Don't stagnate as so many Christians do. Instead, apply 2 Peter 1:5-8 in your life.

REFLECTIONS

....

....

....

....

....

These Are
the Last Days

*Therefore, beloved, knowing this beforehand, be
on your guard lest, being carried away by the
error of unprincipled men, you fall from your own
steadfastness, but grow in the grace and knowledge
of our Lord and Savior Jesus Christ. To Him be the
glory, both now and to the day of eternity. Amen.*

2 PETER 3:17,18

As you prepare for the coming year—
remember Jesus is coming. These are the
last days—difficult times are here. . . . *Therefore,
beloved, knowing this beforehand, be on your
guard . . .*

REFLECTIONS

....

....

....

....

....

Take Inventory

*If you extract the precious from the worthless,
you will become My spokesman.*

JEREMIAH 15:19

*P*recious child of God, as you enter this
new year take inventory of your life, your
ways, your goals, your ambitions.

REFLECTIONS

....

....

....

....

....